D1398909

LEADERSHIP IN THE AGE OF PERSONALIZATION

Why Standardization Fails
in the Age of "Me"

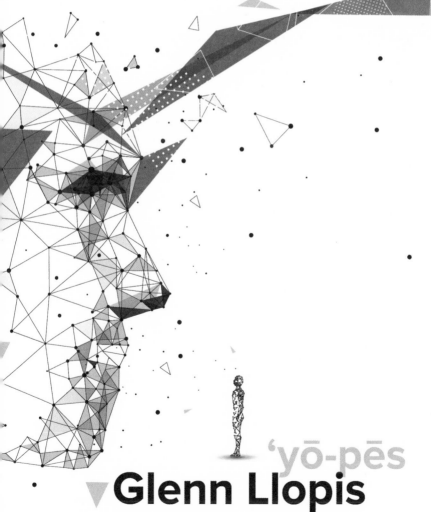

ˈyō-pēs

Glenn Llopis

with Jim Eber

Published and Distributed by GLLG Press
Cover Design: Paulo Silvano, Senior Designer at GLLG
Interior Design: Eliot House Productions
©2019 Glenn Llopis Group, LLC
All rights reserved.

This publication is designed to provide accurate and authoritative information in regard to the subject matter covered.

Library of Congress (LC) Cataloging-in-Publication Data
    Names: Llopis, Glenn, author. Eber, Jim, author (with)
    Title: Leadership in the age of personalization: why standardization fails in the
        age of me / Glenn Llopis with Jim Eber
    Description: Rancho Santa Margarita: GLLG Press, 2019
    Identifiers: LCCN 2019903858 ISBN 978-1-73381-251-1 (hardback)
    Subjects: LCSH: Leadership. Creativity ability in business. Organizational
        change. BISAC: Business & Economics/Leadership
    BISAC Subject Codes: BUS071000, BUS041000 and BUS097000
    LC record available at https://lccn.loc.gov/2019903858

Printed in the United States of America

For my daughter, Annabella Marie Llopis,
and all the leaders of the future

Contents

What Are We Holding Onto?

On December 26, 2004, the third-largest earthquake ever recorded struck the Indian Ocean. Lasting around ten minutes and spanning a fault line more than 800 miles long, the quake had the power of more than 250 megatons of TNT and launched a tsunami that sped hundreds of miles per hour toward the coasts of Indonesia, India, Sri Lanka, Maldives, Thailand, and as far away as Africa. The waves that eventually crashed into those shores—some just hours after the quake started—reached a height of 30 feet and hit with almost no warning. The damage was catastrophic, as was the loss of life: More than 225,000 people died.

Jillian Searle was determined not to count herself and her two young sons, Blake, age 2, and Lachie, age 5, among them.

Jillian and her husband had brought Blake and Lachie to a resort in Phuket from their home in Australia for the holiday to enjoy some of Thailand's most beautiful and popular beaches. And December 26 looked to be a perfect beach day, sunny and calm. Realizing they had forgotten something, Jillian's husband went back into the hotel while she finished getting the boys ready outside. That's when Jillian heard a sound like a jet plane. She saw the birds flying away, and people running past her. Then the water rushed toward them.

Jillian scooped up Blake and grabbed Lachie's hand, and they ran for their lives toward the hotel lobby. They didn't get far before the water overtook them. She held onto her children as the water rushed around them. Unable to fight the force of the water or grab anything while holding both her kids, she realized that if she held onto both children, they would all die. She needed to let one of her sons go. And she knew it had to be Lachie. Lachie was older, stronger, and could swim toward the people reaching out for him just ahead.

So she let her son go.

Jillian never saw what happened to Lachie. She was immediately pulled under, clinging desperately to Blake as the water tossed them. His screams whenever they bobbed to the surface were the only sign he was still alive. They eventually made it to safe ground, and when the water receded Jillian ran back to the hotel to find Lachie. That's when she discovered her son had not made it into those reaching arms. A frantic, desperate search ensued. The worst of all possible thoughts raced through her head—that her unimaginable decision had led to an unimaginable consequence. Then, suddenly, Lachie turned up safe and unhurt right in front of her and said, "Mummy, I'm really dirty. I need a shower."

Most of us will never face life-or-death decisions like Jillian Searle. Certainly few of us will in our businesses. But the growth and health of our people, businesses, and indeed our country depend on our willingness to do what Jillian Searle was able to do in that impossible moment: let go.

We must let go. Not of everything, just the things that fuel our addiction to certainty and prevent us from leading in the age of personalization as the proverbial waters of change rush toward us. Hold onto the need for standards but let go of the need to standardize everything. Hold onto our individuality and let go of what defined us in the past. Hold onto expectations but let go of the need to command and control our people and measure things that are no longer relevant. Hold onto what is human and let go of tribal behavior.

We can't start the work ahead unless we're willing to let go.

PART 1

THE
STANDARDIZATION
OF ME

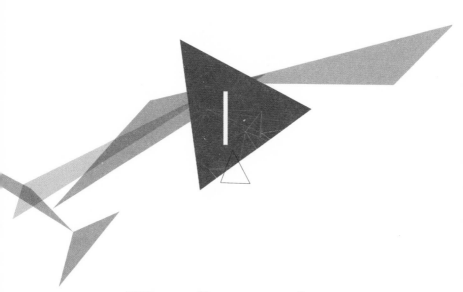

The Scenario

After a change in your organization, two top-performing and well-liked employees who have never met before, have opposing personal beliefs and points of view on seemingly everything, *and* proudly display those beliefs and points of view all around their office spaces end up sitting near each other. Before the change, in all their years neither employee had a complaint made against them nor complained about anyone. Now each has complained about the other to their team leaders and anyone else who will listen. They both say the other's displays, points of view, and beliefs make them uncomfortable, and roll their eyes whenever they cross paths. Human Resources says nothing rises to the level of hate speech or advocating violence, nor has anything cost the company business, so firing one or both employees is not an option right now. But things are getting tense. These are valuable employees who could easily find a job with another company—or with your competitors. The team leaders come to you as their boss to help address the situation. What do you tell them to do?

a. *Ignore the situation.* If it doesn't resolve itself, warn the employees you'll get rid of one or both of them if they can't respect each other.

b. *Move the employees as far away from each other as possible.* Switch them with others if necessary. If it doesn't resolve itself, warn the employees you'll get rid of one or both of them if they can't respect each other.

c. *Make the employee whose beliefs align least with the teams' and/ or company's beliefs take the offending material down.* Use the opportunity to reinforce those beliefs to the teams.

d. *Make both employees take any offending material down.* Create clear rules that limit future office displays to things like family pictures, kids' art, company awards, and kittens or puppies.

e. *Engage the employees—and let them engage each other.* Listen to their stories separately, together, and with their teams. Help everyone understand why individual beliefs and points of view are important—and how those beliefs and the shared beliefs of the company unite all of them.

Choose your answer before proceeding.

The "Right" Answer: Leadership in the Age of Personalization

'm not going out on much of a limb in guessing you chose *e* as your answer to the scenario. More than 85 percent of the leaders I show the scenario to pick *e*, and none of them were reading a book called *Leadership in the Age of Personalization* at the time. I will go one step further and say you and those leaders even believe that *e* is the right answer. You would want to be respected, treated like an individual, and listened to if you experienced a conflict like this. You aspire to treat others this way at work and in life.

I could go on listing reasons that most of us choose *e* and quicker than you can say *I've heard all this before* I'd have a book filled with platitudes—statements that you have heard so many times that they have lost their power to be interesting, meaningful, or motivational beyond a moment: "Think about others' needs!" "Value people as individuals!" "Embrace the power of diversity of thought!"

The problem isn't that these statements have become commonplace or that they aren't the right things to do—they are! Just like *e* is the right answer. The problem is that many leaders have failed—and continue to fail—to execute that answer and drive it through their organizations. Because just believing and knowing that leadership in the age of personalization is the "right" answer is not enough to execute it.

Knowledge and Know-How Affirm What We Already Know

Consider this: Did you need to know more about the circumstances behind the change the organization faced or the specifics of the employees' beliefs and displays in that scenario in order to choose answer *e*? I could have given you those things; I based the scenario on stories from leaders of organizations across multiple industries nationwide, from tech to financial services to health care to retail. The reasons for the changes ranged from mergers to consolidation to corporate restructuring, and the beliefs and points of view covered religion, race, ethnicity, sex, age, sexuality, politics, and more. Would including any of those things in the scenario have changed your answer? Probably not— even if one of the beliefs was toxic to you personally. Since this was not hate speech, nor costing the organization business, most leaders I speak to believe they could listen to another person's differences, no matter how different. They say they could do the business version of what every politician says they want to do while trying to get elected: Reach across the aisle to work together. But that doesn't mean they can actually do it once in office—or in this case, in an office.

You also didn't need to know my definitions of personalization and leadership in the age of personalization to know *e* was the right choice. But here they are now:

▪ Personalization means individuals define the business, as opposed to standardization in which the business defines individuals.

▪ Leadership in the age of personalization builds inclusive systems that actively enable individuals to have the influence to define the business and ensure the organization is welcoming at every level to every individual (that is, "me").

I could provide an avalanche of individual success stories, articles, videos, white papers, books, corporate case studies, and statistics on employee engagement to put these definitions and the power of leadership in the age of personalization in context and show how it leads to a respect for individuality and inclusiveness. Yet you picked *e* without any of that information.

You also picked it without knowing what leaders must do to execute those definitions of leadership in the age of personalization: Elevate and activate individual capacities and account for the realities, stories, and values of themselves, their customers, and their employees. This execution empowers people to be authentic and express their identities without suppressing or siloing the individuality of others. This extends outward from their teams to other teams, departments, divisions, and throughout the organization. Cross-functionality and interdependence are sought and expected across the enterprise. Progress toward individual impact and legacy matter and are measured.

But you didn't need all that to know *e* was right. Nor did you need know-how. I filled my last book, *The Innovation Mentality*, with detailed how-to's for leaders and their organizations to break free from the status quo and value inclusion and individuality. I have delivered hundreds of keynotes, led dozens of executive summits, and worked with thousands of leaders, teams, and organizations before and since that book came out, all of them eager to execute. I laid out clear actionable steps for that execution. "Powerful stuff," they tell me, "we need to act on this!" Then this crisis happens . . . and then the quarterly numbers are off . . . and then the database goes offline . . . and then this client needs their stuff *now* . . . and then they had to fire him . . . and then she quit . . . and then *how much time will this take?*

> *Leader*: Sorry, Glenn I need to reschedule our meeting. I have more important things to deal with right now. Just tell me what I need to do, and I'll try and get it done.

> *Me*: You want me to tell you what to do to lead in the age of personalization and then you'll do what I tell you? Don't you see how that's problematic?

> *Leader*: I'm not sure I understand.

> [Uncomfortable silence.]

Conversations like these speak volumes about why so many leaders and organizations are completely unprepared and unable to execute leadership in the age of personalization, even when they have the knowledge and know-how, see their perspectives are myopic, and believe it's the right thing to do: *They're exhausted.*

A Recipe for the "Right" Answer Is Not Enough

Executing the "right" answer takes vision, time, effort, thought, perseverance, and relationships with your people. But where's the motivation to do all that if no one measures or values you for it, and the culture and systems don't support it? How will employees trust an organization to deliver on the "right" answer if its leaders and the organization can't make it a priority?

When an organization's leaders and their people are consumed by delivering immediate measurable results in the present, their only motivation is to *do*—to comply, check boxes, generate revenue and cut costs, put out fires. That kind of action isn't connected to a lasting commitment. It's not connected to who they are as individuals or what they solve for as leaders, using that information to create best practices for building something bigger, more valuable, and more inclusive and sustainable for the future. It's connected to self-interest and self-preservation—doing what you're told. It's the illusion of progress that is really about reputation management. *It's transactional action that leads to transactional results and growth only in the present.*

That suits many leaders, because most of them learned strategies and developed work habits based on the rules, hierarchies, and metrics of the age of standardization when the business defined the individual. They were told what to do inside the box they were given, had their success measured by results and progress toward the company mission alone, and their department(s) and functionality were fiercely protected and siloed. Given all that, do you really think the majority of today's leaders are ready to engage those two employees in the scenario? Most leaders don't know their employees as individuals or where to begin to execute the "right" answer, and that scares them. They are unprepared to lead in the age of personalization because they are not vulnerable enough to admit they don't know what they don't know. They are also afraid: Leading people through personal conflict is precarious because they fear offending someone, being sued, being out of compliance with HR. Does that sound like you?

Ask yourself honestly: Would you have the relationships and trust in place to bridge the gap between the two colleagues? Do you know your people beyond their job function, title, who they report to, and what you pay them? Do you know them as individuals: their passions, perspectives, personal beliefs, values, and experiences? If you did, nothing in that scenario would have surprised you when the team leaders came to you. In fact, the team leaders wouldn't have come to you because they would know these things too and already would have anticipated the problem and seized it as an opportunity to be inclusive and grow together. But that rarely happens even when leaders know that a culture that supports leadership in the age of personalization will eliminate many of those boxes they're checking. That it can stop fires from starting in the first place. That it can reinforce an organization's commitment to all its people long before scenarios like the one that started this chapter ever occur. Because they can't get out of their own way. Or, rather, out of the way of all of that transactional action that is creating the very chaos leadership in the age of personalization could help manage.

Change and fighting for what's right are hard enough when someone tells you to do it, and they're not what's being measured now. This need for *now* is the main reason so many leaders and organizations that do commit to executing the "right" answer fail to sustain it for very long, even when the benefits are obvious. And they *are* obvious. In my experience, leaders want to know the answer to the one question that matters most to them: *How am I going to grow and keep growing my business in the future?*

As they learn how to lead in the age of personalization, they will find some answers. This kind of leadership attracts and retains the talent and customers you need to grow significantly and sustainably. When an organization drives leadership in the age of personalization up, down, and through its ranks, departments, and divisions, it

- ■ has a rewarding culture, inclusive of *all* people (individuals) you can learn from and who can learn from each other and from you and the organization.
- ■ has a more committed workforce, building impactful and sustainable results that take time to develop but grow more significant as they do.
- ■ has employees who find purpose in what they do and unleash value to the organization.

▪ is prepared for Gen Z—a generation more diverse, personalized, and informed than the Millennials before them—just beginning to enter the workforce, and already with buying power exceeding $500 billion.

You would think leaders would want that for their employees, themselves, and their organizations just in the name of growth, especially employees like the two at odds in the scenario. Remember: The scenario made it clear at the outset the employees were top-performing, well liked, and could work anywhere they wanted. When talent is scarce, everyone would like to think their value would motivate leaders to go beyond self-interest to engage them and their differences. But with leaders unprepared and unable to do that, the pull in the direction of efficiencies, automation, compliance, and doing what you're told becomes even more powerful. Compliance is easier than working toward inclusion. Mission has more value than commitment to individuals and their contributions, their beliefs, and their goals.

This has been my experience with the organizations and leaders most stuck in standardization: When presented with case studies of leaders who have transformed organizations and industries through leadership in the age of personalization and won admiration and imitation by competitors, they still balk at the commitment, because there is no template for how personalization works for their customers, organizations, communities, industries. They focus on the up-front commitment of time and costs, not on how they are offset in the long run with less turnover and more significant, sustainable growth. They stare at the roadmaps I give them while the cultures of their businesses remain the same as they always were, trapped in the failing templates of standardization.

The Future Versus Now

Truth is, I could give most leaders and organizations a GPS for finding their way to the "right" answer of how to lead in the age of personalization, and they would still struggle to execute long term. Because a GPS can't make you want to drive any more than a recipe can make you want to cook. A recipe is information, not motivation. It identifies the ingredients and steps for cooking something, and tells you how long it will take, how it should look, and how it will taste. Throw in a video and a recipe can even show you how to do it. But if you're not used to cooking, it can't motivate and inspire you. You have no deeper emotional connection to the work it takes, and no one is measuring you for the effort. You still might do it once or twice, but eventually you'll stop and fall back into familiar habits. It won't matter in the long run that you know cooking your own food is healthier and more satisfying, and saves money, or that you're cooking for people you care about. If no one values the work it takes to do what you know is right, it's easier to order takeout, microwave a prepared meal, or go to a restaurant and get immediate results without the effort.

In too many organizations, those immediate results have more value than methods that lead to bigger opportunities, bigger results with deeper connections to their people, and bigger growth in the future. Instead, the organization just looks for efficiencies and automation—to get rid of people and to avoid scenarios like this. That's called denial: trying to force standardization tactics into a personalized world. That's what happens when leaders and organizations face the scenario, know the "right" answer, and then refuse to do what Jillian Searle had to do with her son as the waters of the tsunami rushed around her: let go. Let go of something even when everything you have been taught and told says hold on. Let go of standardization that ignores personalization.

It's not that leaders and organizations fail to understand that personalization is right, or even why it is right. It's that they don't see and *feel* why standardization fails in the age of "me"—and how holding onto it is holding them back. As the waters of change rush around them, they fail to have the courage to let go of what is not working, despite fear of the consequences. They continue to hold onto the "wrong" answers.

And here's the kicker: Most leaders are not just holding onto those "wrong" answers; they're executing them in support of the wrong metrics.

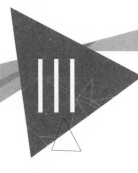

The "Wrong" Answers: Why Standardization Fails

n the age of personalization, tactics designed to make organizations "friendly" to large, impersonal categories of people only succeed in making those people feel unimportant and boxed in. It's not just hot-button identifiers like race, ethnicity, sex, sexuality, religion, age, and politics that get stripped away, but *anything* that defines individual identity. Efforts to group people by the boxes they check similarly fail. Just because someone is, say, Hispanic doesn't mean that person shares buying or working habits with other Hispanics, or anyone else who overlaps with how that person identifies. Every single one of your employees and customers is a mix of preferences and tendencies. Broad categories don't cut it when it comes to individuality.

Given the massive variation of today's workforce and customers, both domestically and globally, leadership in the age of personalization requires this variation to be understood through individual impact and influence. Individual identities and goals must align with shared beliefs in the company's goals and mission. *When you standardize these approaches to "me," you let all individuals define the business: Being human is valued, and variation is expected and encouraged to serve individual and organizational goals.*

But that's only part of why leadership in the age of personalization is important today. It used to be that engagement mattered most. Knowledge and experience counted more than anything else, and we prized creativity and innovation. Today's youngest generations in the workforce (Millennials and Gen Z), and increasingly Gen X and older, look beyond all those things and seek purpose, fulfillment, and identity. That is exactly what the "wrong" standardization answers don't deliver for those two employees in the scenario.

To be clear, most leaders get this. They know and believe that most, if not all, of the first four answers to the scenario are wrong as much as they know the last one is right. Look at the scenario again. The answers—ignore the situation, move the employees away from each other, make one or both employees take the offending material down, and engage the employees—are actually listed in ascending order of the number of leaders who picked them, with less than 2 percent picking "ignore the situation." Yet in reality most leaders and organizations not only ignore situations that need attention, but also do versions of each of the first four answers every day.

Just as knowing something's right isn't enough to start doing it, simply knowing something is wrong isn't enough to stop doing that. And if the first step in solving a problem is defining the problem, then we must see how we persist in doing what we believe and know is wrong. We must see how we're holding onto standardization, understand why it doesn't work, and learn to let go of those parts of it that fail leadership in the age of personalization. Failure to do so exemplifies what I call the *standardization trap*—a trap that happens most when dealing with individuality. **Because personalization spooks standardization, and when threatened, standardization fights back—hard.**

Ignore the Situation

There's a good reason few leaders pick this answer: It's awful. It's the business equivalent of avoiding and refusing to respond to all communication from a boyfriend, girlfriend, or someone interested in you in order to make them go away. It's passive, immature, and in the end ineffective unless your goal is to make one or both of those top-performing employees quit while hating you in the process.

Yet businesses have done this for years to employees when it comes to what I call the Cultural Demographic Shift^{SM} (CDS). CDS is my term for what happens when large cultural segments of the population reach numbers sufficient enough to have a significant effect on what we do and how we act. That is already happening in many parts of the United States; according to the U.S. Census Bureau, our country is projected to become a majority-minority nation in 2043. While the non-Hispanic white population will remain the largest single group, no group will make up a majority. That will be even truer in the workforce as the older workers retire and the latest and next generations—Millennials (those born between the early 1980s and early 2000s) and Gen Z (those born from the early 2000s on)—replace them. These generations are the largest and most ethnically and racially diverse generations ever, many of them the first generation born to immigrants or immigrants themselves. And despite our annoyances with their methods, fixation on social media communications, and the fact that they are *always* wearing earbuds with their eyes on their phones, most studies show they are more driven to earn and more eager to make their mark than the generations before them—and that they want to do it as individuals inclusive of all people.

These future leaders have already started to disrupt not only the way the workforce looks but also the way it *thinks*, with a different view of commitment. Money is important but a paycheck is not enough to stay committed. For them, it's about two questions, questions that matter to *everyone*:

- Do you see me?
- Do you know me?

More and more, we want to be who we are and know we belong, have a purpose, and can contribute to something. We want to have influence and opportunity—and be respected for what we stand for. When these needs are ignored, we are forced to retreat into tribal behavior and associate only with the people, teams, and departments that share our beliefs and points of view. And if we can't find them and the opportunities we seek, we'll leave—which is what Millennials have been doing, faster than any generation before them. Should we have expected them to conform to the standards of the past and wait for opportunities, just like their parents did? To hold onto all they can as the waters of change rush around them? That's not just ignoring a situation—that's ignorance! And it's exactly what Jillian Searle did *not* do in that tsunami. But that's what happens when leaders of the present are unprepared to lead: Their organizations do very little to make their workplaces and office cultures more inclusive to the diverse talent they have worked to attract and retain, to sustain the diversity initiatives designed to attract them—yet the initiatives and thus the organization tend to fail due to a standardized approach.

Too many organizations spend a ton of time and money to get people "in" individually, only to fail them once they arrive by forcing them into existing standards, groups, and teams and not considering their individuality—or anyone else's, but especially those who do not fit into how the organization has always acted and looked. Efforts to understand them as individuals are few and far between, and inclusion initiatives such as employee resource groups and infrequent corporate bonding exercises are simply tactical efforts. Those have their places, but they are still about the business or team defining the individuals. Why would organizations think those efforts are enough to make them inclusive and respectful of individuality without making deliberate and planned changes to their structures, culture, and the mindset of their leaders? Without that change, their efforts are really about compliance, and all individuals—especially but not limited to "diverse" individuals—remain on the fringe of the organization, unable to influence its needs.

Inclusion that reinforces marginalization is not inclusive. Inclusion that is not complemented by efforts to have individual relationships is not personalization. It's a way to ignore the problem under the guise of engagement, togetherness, and team. Let's bring what I mean by that back through the scenario. I agree that sometimes we can be too quick to act when we think something is a problem, and even the best of us can sometimes sweat the small stuff. This scenario was not either of those things, because the leaders—and you—had already ignored the situation. Whatever room there was for individuality in the office, given the displays, nothing had been done to lay the foundation for inclusivity or do more than tolerate individuality while it was not a problem. It was a laissez-faire approach that left exposed just how unprepared leadership was to face challenges once they emerged. That's why the second part of the answer—warn the employees that if things don't change and they can't respect each other, then you'll get rid of one or both of them—is futile. Ask yourself about your employees:

■ Have you shown them that respect by listening to them and understanding them, or just given recognition for their results?

- Have you spoken to them about their beliefs and goals?
- Do you regularly sit with them and coach them through problems, ideas, and opportunities they see or are experiencing?
- Do they know how everyone's individual contribution is going to help the organization grow?
- Have you recently showed genuine gratitude for their work—not just results, but what it takes to get them—even with just a simple thank you?

If you failed to answer yes to any of these questions, you've been ignoring situations and people like the two in the scenario, and your people know it.

Move the Employees as Far Away from Each Other as Possible

Moving the employees only reinforces your ignorance. I think this answer is worse than ignoring the situation, because your solution to the recognition of your ignorance is to sweep it under the rug. Once you do, everything covered in the previous "wrong" answer applies here.

Moving the employees pushes them further away from each other and reinforces tribal behavior, not human interaction and relationships. As the answer says, being willing to switch them with others shows no value for individuality and what makes us human: Everyone must do what is best for the company. The business defines the individual. Standardization rules. *Go team!*

But human beings are not commodities, and we must stop treating them as if they were. Put yourself in the shoes of the employees in the scenario: How would you look at the leaders who thought moving you was the right answer? Would you see any value in who they are and who you are? Would any of the people you were switched with? Leaders need to value their people and *themselves* in order to execute on a commitment to developing new methods for listening, engaging, and understanding individuals to forge relationships and inclusive cultures that enable the trust and sense of belonging from their customers and employees. Moving them further away is just saying "out of sight, out of mind."

Make One or Both of the Employees Take Down Any Offending Material

These are the ultimate "wrong" answers, and hold onto the most corrupt legacies of standardization: While appearing to address the situation, they still ignore it and make executing personalization impossible.

If the leaders and workers of the future want to be who they are, know they belong, have a purpose, and contribute to something, then they must know they can express all that freely. That's what is most important to them, and my group has the data to back that up. We have surveyed more than 14,000 leaders and their employees at small companies all the way up to the Fortune 10. The number one thing employees said they need to act as their authentic selves at work was "a safe environment where no one is judged." Without that safety, there is no incentive to do more than they are told. This safety was twice as important to them as other answers like "feeling valued and respected" or even "trust and transparency from [their] supervisor." Supervisors, however, thought "feeling valued and respected" and "trust and transparency" were the most important. Less than 13 percent of them said that "safe environment free from judgment" was most important. There can be no doubt those things are important, but they flow from "a safe environment where no one is judged," because that's where individuality and inclusion thrive.

That's all those top-performing, long-tenured employees in the scenario wanted. Making them take down expressions of who they are is the exact opposite of that. You might think that creating clear rules that limit future office displays to things like family pictures, kids' art, company awards, and kittens or puppies still allows expression of who they are and what's important to them. *But it's forced assimilation to the mission and rules of the organization. It's command and control—standardization that strips individuals of their identities.*

Mandates to whitewash who people are, instead of being inclusive and respecting individuality, make the business or brand and its goals the number one priority. These are just some of the messages that behavior sends to your people:

- Just get on with the business of the business; the brand is more important than the you.
- Do not question even to understand, just comply; avoid discussing anything that might offend anyone or anything.
- The mission of the company is more important than your individual contribution; you get paid to get results, not to be who you are and do it how you want.

If you like how those sound, you have been corrupted by standardization more than you think. You're either consumed by power and a desire to make people do what you say, or you haven't yet realized that the old ways are failing. Trying to make others comply by minimizing their individuality only minimizes their potential and reinforces your power over their identity. But as I said before, the days of forced assimilation are over even if they still seem to be hanging on. **Unity cannot mean conformity. There's no place for individuality, let alone inclusion, in conformity. No place to understand each other as individuals *and* as employees who share the goals of the company if compliance is the goal.**

Making the employees in the scenario take down anything deemed offensive by corporate standards—like moving them away from each other—only reinforces tribal identities even more, rather than giving them, their teams, and their leaders an opportunity to experience the humanity in each other. Which is exactly what the "right" answer compels leaders to do: Engage the employees—and make them engage each other. Listen to their stories separately, together, and with their teams. Help everyone understand why individual beliefs and points of view are important, and how those beliefs and the shared beliefs of the company unite all of them and lead to that magic word: *growth*. A growth that comes from engagement in spite of the tension it causes.

The Power of Productive Tension

It constantly amazes me how organizations fail to understand this. They get globalization (the world is bigger and more connected than ever before) but fail to understand globalism (shared purpose despite our differences and distinctions). In a global workplace with the coming of the Cultural Demographic Shift, leaders and organizations should understand that some tension is inevitable. None of the "wrong" answers eliminate this tension, however; they just bury it. In a safe environment free from judgment, employees and their leaders can work through that tension productively.

That's what throws most leaders off in the scenario: the tension. The need to avoid conflict. That's the reason more leaders than care to admit choose the answers that involve taking the offending material down: It's the safe compliance play. What these leaders fail to see is that there is productive or healthy tension and unproductive or unhealthy tension. Productive or healthy tension ends with individuals expressing themselves to each other honestly and openly, and shows how shared beliefs in the goals of the company can accommodate their beliefs and give them all significance. It gives them permission to be who they want to be, empowers everyone, and elevates accountability to themselves and others—and across and outside the organization to other teams, departments, divisions, locations, customers, and external partners. This tension is not only productive, but constructively interrupts the way we've been thinking. It allows for vulnerability—a requirement for leading in the age of personalization. Yet still we fail to execute leadership in the age of personalization. Why? Because leadership in the age of personalization requires more than knowledge, new leadership approaches, and letting go of standardization. It requires a new mindset, and mindsets, like all human behavior, are tough to change, even when you know the right thing to do. And we still need to hold onto some of what got us here from the age of standardization.

That's right: While I do think leadership in the age of standardization, as embodied in all the "wrong" answers, is a dinosaur, I don't think standardization is always wrong—or even wrong at all.

That's what leaders and organizations who execute leadership in the age of personalization do differently: They understand not only that personalization is the right answer but also that standardization as a whole is *not wrong*. **Leadership in the age of personalization is not about replacing standardization and personalizing everything—that would be impossible, and lead to mass chaos. It's about *evolving* what standardization does best, to serve personalization.** Do that and you constructively interrupt the way you lead. Do that, and standardization evolves to become more than just part of the age of personalization. It defines it.

IV

Our Next Evolution: The Standardization of Me

heard a story on the radio about the opening of new headquarters of a major consumer products company. The senior executive touted all the things the campus offered: nap rooms and massages, on-site health care and childcare, free lunch with lots of fresh and healthy options, and a state-of-the-art gym. I expected the next sentence would be how all those things empowered employees to be healthier and take control of their health at work. But it wasn't. The next sentence was:

"All these things make the building a personalized experience for every employee because our brand is all about personalization."

Let's be perfectly clear: Those things may satisfy employee expectations and do what I thought in terms of health, but they do not demonstrate leadership in the age of personalization. If they did, employee engagement and talent retention would be off the charts at companies that have all those things. So would consumer engagement and loyalty. They're not. Those amenities may be pieces of what it takes to attract and retain talent and consumers in many businesses and industries today, but in and of themselves they are not about personalization. Nor are they even what I mean by the evolution of standardization. They are modern, state-of-the art approaches to employee and consumer satisfaction, and examples of leadership in the age of standardization.

They are simply the latest example of a line I have been saying since my first book, *Earning Serendipity*: Without strategy, change is merely substitution not evolution.

Standardization, Unevolved

Gyms and on-site health care may demonstrate awareness of employee demands and needs today, but they don't change the culture of the company, make it more inclusive, or necessarily reflect and allow employee influence. They are not tools for the engagement, listening, relationships, sense of belonging, and safe environments free from judgment required to execute leadership in the age of personalization. Think back to the scenario: Would the availability of the best treadmills for both employees at work solve for the tension between them? Would leaders expect them to hug it out over free salad and flu shots?

While that senior executive at the consumer products company missed the mark with understanding that connection to standardization, most employees don't. They get that those things are tools for keeping them happy and satisfied and around at work when work-life balance is illusory. The perks checked off by that senior executive are just that: transactional benefits offered by the business to satisfy certain employee expectations, similar to a paycheck. Not unimportant or unnecessary, but all about the business defining what it thinks individuals want, not about individual employees having influence. And those things don't need to be all things to all individuals. Because leadership in the age of personalization is not about being all things to all individuals, but about *accommodating* individuality.

The problem isn't that the gym exists, but the idea that it solves for leadership in the age of personalization. Think of it this way: If you were building a gym at your company, would you go to every single employee, ask what they need and do for a workout, and then make sure everything mentioned was available in the gym whether 100 people asked for it or just one? Of course not. That's customization and it's a recipe for chaos. It would need to be adjusted every single time a new employee started or an old one left. A gym should be modern, welcoming, standardized, *and* personalized—designed to appeal to the most employees possible and to make everyone feel like the company was at least paying attention and gave them influence over how it worked. One would hope the company I heard the story about did that: surveyed its employees and the market and created a gym that offered most of what people asked for, from equipment to trainers and classes, and not just what the senior executives wanted or thought the employees wanted. An organization that practices leadership in the age of personalization would get honest answers back from that survey and create a gym—and in future, any employee benefits—that reflected the feedback of *all* its employees. It would also be sure not to judge employees who choose to go to their own gym. Or choose when they go, or even don't go to a gym. Or like to swim or run outside and don't use gyms. Or like to do tai chi in the park. Or work out in private because they are modest. Or refuse to have meetings and conversations at the office gym during their workouts because that's where they go to unwind alone. . . .

IV / our next evolution: the standardization of me

That's what it means to accommodate individuality in the age of personalization. In the age of standardization, no organizations took this into account. Everyone had to work and do things in the same manner, and the people and floorplans basically looked the same: offices for the leaders, cubicles or shared offices for the worker bees, and desks outside the offices for the secretaries. Then many companies went to open plans, ostensibly to break down the walls between people, positions, and departments, and to prompt collaboration. They didn't. Today, many organizations have realized that no one way works. Individuals work differently, and while any floor plan and fixed hours may work for many people, they don't for everyone. Companies need to give options—from flex hours to telecommuting to spaces for privacy—when needed.

So when it comes to physical space and time, leaders have realized that they can be deliberate with design in order to give people as many ways as possible to individualize the way they work. They can still do that within the basic structure of the building and let individuals define the way they work without creating chaos. They have standardized their approaches to the personalization of space and time. But not of people. Removing the physical walls doesn't remove the mental barriers or change the culture of the company any more than a gym does. Just consider stories about how tech firms of today have frat-house cultures that act and look like the 1960s and the TV show *Mad Men*. They're supposedly more modern and progressive, but still lead like the age of standardization, failing to be inclusive of women and many of the populations in the workplace they serve as customers. Thus, the "right" answer to the scenario is still elusive.

Leaders and their organizations don't need a new office building to execute leadership in the age of personalization. They need a new mindset about standardization and what it means to lead and work in the age of "me." Enter the standardization of "me," which holds onto the best parts of leadership from the age of standardization, lets go of the rest, and evolves what's left to accommodate and execute on the individuality and inclusion valued by leadership in the age of personalization.

The Evolution of Personalization: The Standardization of Me

In the past, variation spooked standardization, which is why personalization spooked standardization. It shouldn't, and we know better now and even expect it—at least as customers. When we are purchasing any service or product—groceries, clothing, cars, mortgages, meals in a restaurant, and anything else you can think of—our experiences and feelings of satisfaction are lifted by people and organizations that value our needs as individuals, listen to the problems we are having, and ask questions to understand those things. We expect this of "smart" products that dominate our homes and are designed to answer our questions as well as learn from us, adapt to how we live, and be customized to suit any situation. Why do you think companies are investing billions in algorithms, AI, and digital transformations to determine what you want and need to see, will like, should buy, and must do? The products themselves may be limited to certain choices, but not the software aimed at making our lives easier, safer, and better. This extends to the entire marketplace for goods and services. It extends to patients needing attention from a clinic, doctor's office, or hospital to telemedicine to medication consults at a pharmacy. It extends to parents choosing paths, schools, and programs for their children. It even extends to the biggest corporate mergers and deals.

As I wrote this book, Amazon's deal for one of its new headquarters in New York City fell apart largely because it failed to understand the city and its people and make a genuine effort to understand the market. From the start of the process, the company lacked transparency and deemed unimportant the work of understanding how the city worked. It never made an effort to listen to the people and community it would impact. In other words, Amazon failed to execute the "right" answer from the scenario when it came to engaging New York City: "Listen to their stories separately, together, and with their teams. Help everyone understand why individual beliefs and points of view are important—and how those beliefs and the shared beliefs of the company unite all of them." That this did not seem to matter to the other location Amazon chose for its headquarters (where the company experienced no deal-breaking resistance to its announcement) is not proof that this does not matter, just that it does not matter there *now*. Who knows how many bad feelings or problems could be avoided down the road if the "right" answer was in place from the beginning?

The Amazon example is just the biggest of countless examples of customers and employees wanting to be listened to, understood, and treated as individuals, or at least feel they have been. Even if it's just a feeling when entering a store or office, clicking on a website, or starting an online chat or phone call, we want to feel like we matter—that our identities are important. We may lose patience when we wait too long to get help or find what we need. But we lose *trust* when we feel the business and the people who work there don't care, are following a script, or don't try to understand us as individuals. When leaders and organizations simply want us to follow directions and comply with how they work, and find as many ways as possible to ignore us for as long as possible when we have a problem, we feel like they just want us to go away. No feeble attempts at engagement like employee suggestion boxes or annual town halls will overcome that.

Not to sound too much like *Jerry Maguire,* but too many companies lose their people—and their customers—at hello. From there, they grow increasingly frustrated, disengaged, and distrustful of motives and missions. Which is why you, your team leaders, and your employees at the company in the scenario, like Amazon in New York City, *already lost* before choosing that answer: You lost them at hello. If you and the leaders in the scenario had been focused on forging relationships with people, understanding their values and differences, respecting their methods, coaching them, holding regularly scheduled one-on-one meetings, and questioning the organization to understand how changes at the company would affect its people so you can move them along together, then there likely never would have been a scenario.

Because the standardization of "me" empowers the execution of the "right" answer from the scenario up, down, across, and outside the organization from the moment it is enabled. It standardizes systems, processes, and metrics for an organization to make individuality and inclusion not just *a* priority, but *the* priority.

The biggest reasons we need standardization—rules, regulations, smart systems—are as clear in business as they are in life.

- We know what is expected.
- We have clear goals and deliverables.
- We can be efficient and avoid mass chaos.
- We never lose focus on generating results.

Those things shouldn't undermine individuality, inclusion, and leadership in the age of personalization. They're just not what most company's key performance indicators (KPIs) and metrics are set up to measure. Moreover, those things are not enabled or replaced by automation, AI, or digital transformation, if only because human behavior is really hard to standardize and automate—at least for very long. Even the latest advances will be more standardized substitution if they are not directed by leaders and humans toward *all people*—toward the standardization of "me."

Executing that, however, requires a human touch that thinks about people as a mosaic of individuality (individual tiles of "me" combined to make a brilliant picture) not a melting pot (in which individual differences are stripped away in the name of forced assimilation and standardization to the norm). Standardization suppressed those individual identities in the name of serving the mission of the brand or organization. In return for the business defining who they were and how they acted, those individuals got job security and a steady paycheck that allowed them to live what used to be called the American Dream. This is not the same dream in the age of personalization. The standardization that lives on from that age can't accommodate individuals who want more: to belong, have a purpose, and contribute without feeling judged.

Leadership in the age of personalization and the standardization of me can. The age of standardization was about the standardization of *us*. **The standardization of me is a mindset that reinforces the balance between standardization and personalization.**

A New Mindset for Standardization

I have been part of and worked with some of the largest organizations in the world across almost every industry from health care to automotive from big-box retail to banking. I have heard what people are thinking but not saying to their leaders: We have been conditioned to operate in environments that standardized our identities and now we want those identities back. But as I said before, corporate values and mission statements never account for the mass variations of this need for individuality and inclusion and the coming of the Cultural Demographic Shift—even when they say they do. That's why they are unprepared for the standardization of me. Saying—and even believing—*we respect individuals* or *we value and strive for diversity and inclusion* is not execution of those beliefs. Substituting even more inclusive words every few years but never challenging anyone to do the evolved *thinking* needed to live those values and mission statements does not lead to employee influence either, just as a gym does not lead to a mindset of personalization; it only reinforces the mission of the company over inclusion and individuality.

Again, think back to the scenario: Would writing "we love and serve our people" mean everyone was doing it? Would it be enough to engage and retain those two employees? No, and it's not enough to engage your people, either. Even if they don't quit, they will disengage, and we have all heard the statistics on how disengaged our workforce is and how that disengagement costs us billions every year. It's not just the vast majority of Millennials who are disengaged either; nearly half of the generations before them report being disengaged at work. That's right: The very leaders who reinforce the rules from the age of standardization feel alienated by it. Yet senior leadership still fights the evolution to leadership in the age of personalization out of fear—the fear of being vulnerable and exposing their insecurities about how little they understand what needs to be done, and their inability to lead through change. That's why so many leaders today are unprepared to lead this transformation even if the mission of the company says they should. Because corporate missions are about standardization; they are about attitude. Shared beliefs are about personalization and align around individual and organizational goals; they are about *mindset*. Shared beliefs allow for alignment between the goals of the company and the goals of individuals.

As I finished writing those words in the last few paragraphs, I experienced a powerful feeling of déjà vu I initially could not place. And that's when it hit me: This is exactly what I was talking about as the difference between "corporate values" and "shared beliefs" in my last book, *The Innovation Mentality*. Only then I was discussing the line between "substitution" words and "evolution" words. I didn't see it then, but the substitution words were all about standardization and the evolution words were all about personalization. Here are a few of them.

Substitution/Standardization	Evolution/Personalization
Compliance	Commitment
Control	Influence
Managing	Relationship
Corporate Values	Shared Beliefs

Substitution/Standardization	Evolution/Personalization
Differences	Distinction
Recognition	Respect
Connection	Alignment
Responsibility	Expectation
Success	Significance

Note in that list that the standardization words are not always bad, or even negative. The first three (compliance, control, and managing) have the strongest negative associations for most leaders but the last four (recognition, connection, responsibility, and success) have largely positive associations. But I don't think any of them are right or wrong just limited and limiting legacies of the age of standardization. That's what I really want you to do: **stop thinking of words as bad or good; think of them as limiting or unlimiting**. Connection is important, and companies must have clearly stated values. But they are means to an end. Finite. Limited. Unevolved. Impersonal. Exclusive. Traps. They are why standardization fails us in the age of "me" by making leaders and organizations

- ■ focus on diversity, not solve for inclusion.
- ■ focus on recognition that leads to tribalism, not human respect.
- ■ focus on controlling individuality and having everyone serve the brand/company, not understanding individual identities and capacities.
- ■ focus on mission and compliance, not the contribution and influence of individuals.
- ■ focus on managing transactional results that lead to success, not empowering people to discover challenges and projects, and to connect and collaborate to achieve success *and* significance.

Start to shift your mindset by understanding a new set of word pairings.

Leadership in the Age of Standardization	Leadership in the Age of Personalization
Diversity	Inclusion
Tribal	Human
Brand Identity	Individual Identities
Mission	Contribution
Results	Methods

Letting go of the words under the Age of Standardization and standardizing the words under the Age of Personalization is how we get the standardization of "me." A deeper dive into why and how we must do that follows in this book. In each chapter, I'll lay out the whys for

- shifting your mindset away from the standardization word and toward the personalization word;
- finding new approaches to the way we value personalization;
- avoiding the traps of standardization; and
- preparing for digital transformation, industry consolidation, and operational excellence in the age of "me."

But before I do, let me say one last thing: I get it. Reinvention is exhausting—perhaps more exhausting than the chaotic work leaders are doing now, which is just doing what they're told. Better to fight and resist rather than to recognize that we have to think differently about the way we approach our work and how work works . . . and who we are! One senior leader told me after slogging through the chaos during two decades at her company that she didn't have the will to change anymore. She also admitted that it annoyed her that changing now would mean the next generation wouldn't have the same slog she did. But then she thought from a more human side and considered all the questions I've been asking since the start of the book. And then she said: *I should want them to go through that simply because I did, and be as tired as I am? I should want them to lose a sense of who they are just because I had that stripped away from me? I should wait for the company to value what they bring to the table and it's too late for me to contribute?*

Those revelations from that leader who had seen her identity stripped away over the course of two decades are exactly why none of this works in your head unless you know in your heart what I am telling you: Operationalize this or fail to lead in the future. You are running out of time. If you don't reinvent yourself and your organization, you will become extinct—or at least your role will.

Experience has less and less value these days. Most skills can be automated, some might say commoditized. That's the problem with standardization in the age of personalization: everything begins to lose value, importance, and relevance faster. Standardization and the efficiencies that go with it should give us the time to invest in leadership in the age of personalization to make organizations and their leaders relatable and relevant now and in the future. It's time to do more than think about what this means, not only to the health of our economy but to ourselves. It's time to be the best *me* and *us* we can be. It's time to let go and embrace the standardization of "me!"

PART 2

STANDARDIZATION:
DIVERSITY
PERSONALIZATION:
INCLUSION

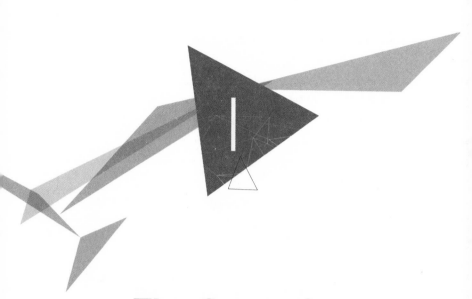

The Scenario

Your organization has tasked you with its expansion into a market where its goods and services are badly needed, but it has no footprint and limited name recognition. The population of the region is very diverse but largely Hispanic, specifically Mexican American and Central American. You have no connections to this market, nor are you Hispanic. You have, however, been given the opportunity to hire your right hand: the person who will lead the expansion for you on the ground. This person will be immediately responsible for assembling a team, increasing brand awareness, and connecting with leaders in the communities. That last part is key: Working with local leaders in those communities and governments is essential to your success in the area, which by all counts doesn't trust newcomers quickly.

The company preference is for a diverse hire, but with no internal candidate for the position, you have narrowed the choice down to two candidates. Both are women. Both around the same age. One is a Mexican American who has lots of experience in the industry but has never lived or worked anywhere near the market and has no knowledge of the target audience. The other is a white non-Hispanic who has less industry-specific experience but has lived and worked in the target market all her life and is well established in the local business and broader communities.

Who would you hire, and why? Take a moment to answer before continuing.

What Are We Solving For: Diversity or Inclusion?

Based solely on the information presented here, one candidate better represents a choice for leadership in the age of personalization; the other, standardization. The majority of the senior leaders (nondiverse and diverse) I present this scenario to pick the Mexican-American woman. She represented diversity and the diverse hire the company asked for. She had the industry experience. It's usually at this point, as they go deeper into explanations of these reasons, that they sense my silence and say, "Uh-oh, I'm wrong, aren't I?" *Yes.* Because the Mexican-American woman solves for exactly what the organization wanted: diversity (that is, optics and workforce representation) and experience (a résumé that matches the job title and description). *And diversity and experience don't solve for inclusion. They reinforce standardization.*

Let's consider experience first. Say an organization needs to hire someone to lead a product division. So they bring in candidates who have had experience in leading that type of product or related industry divisions and exclude all others. Because that's what was valued in the past. Because that's what they were told and taught to do. That's the age of standardization talking. Don't get stuck there: *let go.*

What's the Matter with Experience?

I concede experience of some kind should be taken into account and can be important in some cases, like filling a short-term need in an unfamiliar area (legal work, accounting, setting up new technology). Experience when it comes to qualifications also matters when it comes with knowledge that can affect lives (you don't hire a chief of surgery who has never been in an operating room) or can lead to chaos (a foreman who has never walked a factory floor). But in most cases, experience is about allegiance to hierarchies, leaders' need to protect their status and the status quo, and our desires to control people, compete with others, and insist on being the experts. It's born out of fear: If we hire someone and they don't work out, we can point to their qualifications and say, "How was I to know?" It's also lazy: It requires no thought beyond checking the right boxes.

For those trying to get hired or promoted, knowing we have to have the exact right mix of items on our résumés makes us feel like we have to be good at the things we've been told to be good at. So it removes our motivation to develop skills that haven't been declared desirable by the bosses. It squashes our individuality and it teaches us to squash the individuality of others.

When hiring, ask yourself:

- How much does most experience, especially industry-specific experience, really matter?
- How much is about time served and how much is about the ability to do the job?
- What are the skills that come with that experience that *can't* be taught?
- What is the focus on that experience blinding you to?

Let me help you answer that last question: You're probably blind to an individual's capacity to contribute. You're probably neither seeing nor understanding the value of the other kinds of qualifications that are as important—or more important. If you only hire people with the same work experience, you're not shifting your mindset and opening up to the possibility of new thinking. You're hiring people who probably already think like you do. Consider the scenario: I never said work experience mattered. What mattered most was knowledge of the community and the individual connections essential for creating trust and engagement in a market that "doesn't trust newcomers quickly." The nondiverse candidate had those relationships. The Mexican-American candidate had the industry experience and, of course, she looked like the target market. She solved for diversity. Does that mean the other candidate, by virtue of how she looked, did not? Either candidate can certainly build a diverse team around her. It's not a huge mental stretch that the nondiverse candidate, by virtue of her relationships and in spite of her appearance, would have the ability to find qualified diverse local hires to connect the organization even deeper in the communities. Yet most leaders chose experience. That's perpetuating a system that is exclusive, not inclusive. **Because diversity distracts us from inclusion, even though we link the two words in our organizations and our heads. That's how we get stuck in the standardization trap of diversity.**

Diversity Does Not Solve for Inclusion

Diversity is a logical first step in solving for inclusion: An organization starts by counting what it has in order to understand what it lacks. It then uses that to standardize approaches and solve for more of the "thems" it needs (in the case of the scenario, hiring the Mexican-American woman to reach people who check the same box as her). But what happens after it achieves diversity? Diversity does not automatically lead to inclusion. Those who were hired for diversity know it. And they feel it. They feel separate because of it, not included.

I'm not saying ignore diversity; I'm saying it's meaningless if that's where you stop. Diversity solves for workforce representation and quotas, compliance and reputation management. **Diversity solves for the standardization of *them* and *us*. Inclusion solves for the standardization of me *and* us.**

- Inclusion is a *behavior* that opens our minds to the importance of being more interconnected and interdependent with each other—within our departments and across the enterprise. When we act in a way that elevates another person's individuality, rather than trying to get them to be or think just like we do, that action opens our minds to the importance of being more interconnected and interdependent.
- Inclusion is an active system for making sure the organization is welcoming at every level, to every individual.

Solving for diversity without solving for inclusion inevitably leads to forced assimilation and the command-and-control leadership mindset that is a hallmark of the age of standardization. This can happen in even the most progressive organizations and in organizations that were created to provide opportunities for those normally not included at the proverbial table. Consider these three stories that appeared as I wrote this book:

- Google announces plans to hire more female engineers, with a goal of achieving a 50-50 male-female balance—up from the current split of 80 percent male/20 percent female. As part of its plan, the company partners with (among others) the National Girls Collaborative Project, which creates programs designed to foster the next generation of female engineers.

■ After a Starbucks employee at one of their Philadelphia stores calls the police on two black men for sitting and waiting for a meeting, and their subsequent arrest for refusing to leave when asked, the company drops all charges against the men, meets with them, issues a public apology, and declares it will close more than 8,000 of its stores nationwide for an afternoon of antibias training. About 175,000 employees participate in the program, guided by former CEO Howard Schultz and activist-musician Common and developed with the help of the NAACP and the Anti-Defamation League.

■ Former New York City Mayor Michael Bloomberg donates $1.8 billion in scholarship money for low-income students at Johns Hopkins University. It is the largest gift to any academic institution in U.S. history.

Chances are you remember one if not all of those stories. They commanded attention in the national media and rightly so: They were big actions taken by two big organizations and one billionaire in three different industries (technology, retail, and higher education) to address inequalities, discrimination, and diversity with women, African Americans, and low-income students, respectively. And I applaud them. At the very least, the companies offered more than the typical lip service and token promises to address the situations. The question is: *What are they solving for: diversity or inclusion?*

These initiatives solve for diversity (such as women, African Americans, and low-income students). And diversity is important. But what's even more important is what happens next. If Google, Starbucks, and Johns Hopkins don't figure out inclusion, employees, customers, and students at countless other companies and institutions remain diversity "problems" that must be solved. Their leaders will see diversity as cost centers, not growth opportunities. That's the age of standardization talking—and it talks a lot, at too many companies, whether they admit it or not.

Thinking about the scenario and the three news stories, ask yourself honestly: How much of what you do when it comes to diversity and inclusion is about compliance and how much is about seizing an opportunity for growth? How much is because you *have to*, and how much is because you genuinely *want to*? Even when leaders and their organizations say they are on the side of growth and wanting to, their words often mix in some sense of compliance and having to. Most of them don't know any other way: **Most organizations are not built for inclusion and individuality.**

The Starbucks PR nightmare following its Philadelphia story and similar stories in the age of *#MeToo* and more have forced organizations to critically evaluate their diversity and inclusion initiatives, lest they find themselves in a similar situation. This is especially true at public companies, organizations looking for investors or to break into new markets, and businesses seeking to attract more diverse customers and employees as the Cultural Demographic Shift approaches. In other words, pretty much everyone. When an employee or customer "problem" becomes public, they rush to announce one-off diversity programs and standards, such as hiring initiatives, community outreach programs, antibias and sensitivity trainings, employee resource groups, and donations to charities that promote equality and social justice. These platforms seem to say "We are dealing with the problem. We will represent you." But do they? Most often not. They make you *think* that, but when the bad news cycle goes away and shareholder attention subsides, diversity gets addressed and inclusion and individuality—and thus personalization—remain unsolved for.

Because diversity does not connote individuality: a concerted effort to know and account for the realities and the values of individual employees and customers. Because diversity does not ensure that the organization is welcoming at every level to every individual. Because diversity does not solve for inclusive systems that actively enable individuals to have the influence to define the business.

Because diversity is about standardization.

Diversity: First Steps and Next Steps

et's go back to the three news stories and consider them the way I did the scenario that opened this part: as first steps into a community in which the organization lacks representation. The real test for these and any organization is understanding why it must move from diversity to inclusion and why it often fails to think about the most impactful next steps: the strategy for change, not the tactics.

The real test for Google isn't just finding the female engineers now or grooming future female engineers. Recruitment is diversity. Inclusion requires a culture that breeds individuality and the influence that comes from it. While famously liberal, Silicon Valley also has a famously male "bro" culture that not only is disrespectful of women but also refuses to deal with that disrespect, especially the pay inequality between men and women. Reports of sexual harassment at Google, how that harassment has always been seen but not spoken about at the company, and how one of the accused harassers even resigned over the charges but got a $90 million exit package with no mention of the accusations led engineers at Google to organize a company-wide "women's walk" walkout. Will this compel Google's leadership to shift its mindset and be more inclusive?

The real test for Starbucks will be taking the learnings from their four-hour antibias training and driving it through the organization and its stores to bridge the gap between the standardization of "them" and the standardization of "me." It takes time to change human behavior and the culture of an organization. Will Starbucks do the ongoing work to shift its mindset and make itself inclusive?

The real test for Johns Hopkins is not only finding the low-income students they do not now serve and convincing them to apply and then come once they get in, but focusing on what happens once the students arrive. Low-income, minority, and first-generation students are not well represented at Johns Hopkins today, or in higher education in general. What will they see and feel when they get there? Will the school expect them to act like everyone else? Will the security guards and staff see them as students or as "others"? A free ride doesn't lead to inclusion any more than it leads to graduation, which is already a big problem— especially for lower-income students—at many schools. According to the National Center for Education Statistics, higher-income students (from families earning $90,000 a year or more) have a 50 percent chance of getting a degree by age 24. For families earning less than $35,000?

That chance falls to less than 6 percent. Will Johns Hopkins adopt a new mindset to transcend this, where other universities have failed?

Diversity Rights and Wrongs

In the political and public life of the United States today, inclusion can feel like a quaint, impossible concept. If it feels like our country has become more divided along race, gender, and other lines, that's because it has. According to the Haas Institute at the University of California, Berkeley, the United States has not only become less inclusive, but also declined in inclusivity compared with all other countries since 2016. But we didn't need UC Berkeley to tell us that. Listening to and reading the news, and watching our social media feeds, it can be hard to imagine our world is anything but fractured.

Will our businesses and global institutions follow suit? C-suite leaders say they understand that for their organizations to survive and thrive in a world in which their employees and customers span multiple countries, languages, generations, cultures, and socioeconomic backgrounds, they need to be inclusive. But just because those organizations have increasingly diverse workforces—and our population is on the cusp of a Cultural Demographic Shift led by Gen Z—doesn't mean everyone is included, able to be individuals, have influence, or contribute to growth.

Yes, we all understand—perhaps more now than ever—that people come from diverse backgrounds, but why must we continue to define them by their ethnicity, race, gender, and other factors usually lumped under diversity? That creates a "them not us" approach, which is how most of our corporate diversity programs operate: by putting people in boxes and counting them. This is why leaders and organizations too often fail to see that diversity without inclusion works against personalization—and that failure extends beyond individuals to teams and departments, and works to further silo them by undermining cross-functionality. *Diversity: the ultimate standardization trap.*

Diversity and the Failure of Leadership

Let me reemphasize something I said in *The Innovation Mentality*: The irresponsible use of the word *diversity* by businesses over the years has forever linked it to politically charged agendas that make people feel uncomfortable and drives them into silos. It also promotes a compliance mindset. A compliance mindset happens when organizations place an emphasis on ensuring that diversity initiatives are in place to celebrate employee differences. That does not solve for inclusion. Inclusion is the platform for leveraging the intellectual capital in all people, to make better decisions and drive business growth. Inclusion connects individual capacity, capability, and purpose with the needs of the organization regardless of hierarchy or rank, department affiliation, and/or experience. But that will never happen if those responsible for inclusion are limited to diversity and inclusion officers and Human Resources departments that manage cost centers, lack business acumen, and are stuck in standardization that makes people feel judged, not valued. Is that what will happen at Google, Starbucks, Johns Hopkins, and any organization launching a big, bold diversity initiative? Who will lead the charge once the inclusion work begins? If the organization is executing leadership in the age of personalization, the answer—and the expectation—is: everyone. Individuals work to change the culture to be more inclusive and welcoming to all, and to attract and retain the talent that diversity initiatives bring in. Inclusion is a skill we all have to learn. The next question is: Who organizes that? The answer should be Human Resources. But few departments in any organization are more stuck in the age of standardization than HR.

HR *should* be a leader when it comes to leveraging diversity to serve individuality and inclusion. After all, it's the only department that's solely dedicated to touching human capital across the organization. Investing in the standardization of me should have started a long time ago and HR should have led it. Yet most HR programs, especially those linked to diversity and inclusion:

- lack a growth mindset by being compliance driven (important, but not about growth)
- solve for performance metrics linked to the age of standardization (important, but not about individuality).

As a result, with the need for individuality and inclusion reaching an all-time high, HR is often ill equipped to execute strategies linked to personalization. Why did this happen? Because organizations thought that standardization was stronger than personalization. They miscalculated the power of individuality. They thought that assimilation and command-and-control should prevail. They ignored the influence of globalization. They made HR-grounded diversity initiatives about compliance, to enable corporations to better defend themselves against employee discrimination lawsuits and to blame individuals for violations of them, especially if the employees were not aware of the initiatives, policies, and guidelines (which no one reads or understands). As a result, when organizations need to account for diversity, the first step HR takes is usually tactical: initiatives managed separately in various silos of the organization, all based on achieving compliance. Most HR executives and their teams have not evolved fast enough—if at all—to see that all these diversity initiatives are solving for is compliance or standardization, not for personalization and certainly not for inclusion. They don't see that **inclusion and individuality can solve for compliance *and* growth.**

I get why this happened. Inclusion requires people up and down the organization—not just HR—to be expert in people, no matter what function they lead. That is not easy to measure and track, because the metrics from the age of standardization were never designed for personalization. Start shifting your thinking by asking these questions: *Do you promote cross-functional cooperation? Do you embrace the unique ways individuals think, act, and desire to influence? Do you adopt inclusion-based corporate cultures that promote readiness for change?*

If your title is Chief People Officer, you should be energized by the fact that your expertise is central to your organization's success in an age of personalization. You should also be feeling some pressure: If a non-HR leader can answer those questions "Yes!" and activate inclusion and individuality by consciously leading with personalization, then this could create natural competition for HR. This competition would hopefully be seen as a powerful and inspiring opportunity to forward-thinking HR people who will exclaim, "Yes, we can own this across the organization. We're experts in this!" Meanwhile, HR people stuck in the current norm of standardization will see it as a threat, perhaps never realizing they'd better evolve and change their strategy. They will become obsolete as their compliance jobs move into legal or get outsourced. They will never grow.

Compliance is important, but inclusion shouldn't be confined to a tactical, functional area. It should be part of a growth strategy that everyone embraces, and that influences how they interact with and engage with others both internally and externally. Think of it this way: When people decide to share a home, or a life together, have babies, adopt children, or have aging parents move in with them, should they expect the "norm"—the status quo—to serve them well, as it has in the past? Would you demand everyone adapt to how you live? No, you'd recognize the need to let go of how things have always been, and evolve to create something new. You'd see it as an opportunity for growth.

So why is it so hard to see this with inclusion in the workplace?

Inclusion Is a
Growth Strategy

Organizations that make employees and customers feel included on an individual level will have a huge advantage over those that don't. But that takes a concerted, *strategic* effort, and many organizations are not making that effort. They haven't yet put inclusive behaviors and systems into action. Because they have no strategy for inclusion; they only have tactics for diversity.

When it comes to diversity, organizations can have both a strategy (Google's plan to even the number of male and female engineers) and tactics that support that strategy (their partnership with the National Girls Collaborative Project). The more varied your tactics, the better chance you have of achieving your strategic goals. Unfortunately, the diversity tactics that organizations take usually don't follow any defined strategy beyond "react and count," let alone go far enough to comprise a strategy for inclusion. With no underlying strategy, these tactics rarely lead to retention or sustainable change, because they reflect leadership in the age of standardization: reactive efforts linked to compliance and reputation management. That's what Starbucks's antibias training was: an immediate and well-meaning—but still reactive and tactical—mea culpa of compliance. Not a strategy for change. *And without strategy, change is merely substitution, not evolution.*

Inclusion can be that strategy for change and growth: whatever goals the organization has set in order to grow the business today and to be ready for what will be needed to grow the business in the future.

Leading Inclusion as a Growth Strategy

Seeing inclusion as a growth strategy requires having systems and processes in place to enable inclusion throughout the enterprise in ways that are measurable and attainable. Growth then depends on the ability and willingness of employees to learn new skills, stretch themselves, and take on new challenges. That makes inclusion essentially a new skill. So the question is: How to measure all this?

As my organization has experienced firsthand, introducing new performance metrics is often met with resistance because it requires the entire organization, including its leaders, to reevaluate existing metrics and systems. If you worked hard to "score" and "win" against the old metrics, assessments, and KPIs, and structured your career trajectory according to them, then any change to those metrics might feel like having the rug pulled out from under you. Which is why change is hard, and hard for most leaders to accept. To empower leaders to do this across the enterprise, why not turn to the very department that has grown most complacent with the old metrics in the age of standardization: HR. Why not challenge HR to develop the tools to standardize "me" and constructively interrupt thinking? Let them serve the organization, as so many already long to do.

- HR could use people analytics to reveal trends that measure decision making and teamwork in new ways that drive growth.
- HR could ensure that people are able to be their whole selves and don't have to hide aspects of themselves from leaders or coworkers (regardless of hierarchy or rank).
- HR could establish employee feedback loops and knowledge-sharing processes to ensure their ability to influence growth strategies and that no one gets stuck in silos. (Remember: inclusion that reinforces silos or marginalization is not inclusive.)

But let's be clear: none of this happens without organizations, their leaders, and their employees having the ability to be authentic and to respond to others being authentic without the fear of judgment. An inclusive culture embraces individuality, and a culture of individuality can lead to inclusion. But note: Neither guarantees the other. Attitudes and mindsets reflect actions. If you're encouraged to "be yourself" but not given any opportunity to contribute "yourself" to the success of the company, then that encouragement is useless. And vice versa: If you're encouraged to contribute but not allowed to be yourself, then your organization is not being inclusive or encouraging individuality. This goes beyond cultural, gender, and/or generational differences. This is about everyone in an organization taking ownership and committing themselves to getting to know their employees, coworkers, and consumers as individuals. It's about creating strategies that serve the like-mindedness within those differences, rather than defining people by them.

Think about inclusion the way you view innovation. You might take a functional approach, funding a state-of-the-art innovation lab and a team of experts to explore innovative ideas full time. There are upfront costs associated with innovation, but you also know that enabling true innovation will pay off over time. You may also want an innovative spirit to permeate the organization. An enterprise that truly values innovation will want people at all levels and in all departments to learn how to be innovative.

Inclusion is no different. You need people at all levels to learn how to be inclusive. And you need an "inclusion lab"—HR or another department—to take responsibility for making sure that inclusion is a skill developed at every level, just like innovation or leadership skills. Easier said than done. My organization's research and assessments of thousands of leaders across industries found a lack of readiness among those leaders eager to lead inclusion as a growth strategy. For example, only 52 percent of leaders and organizations in consumer packaged goods, 56 percent in financial services, and 57 percent in health care were prepared to lead inclusion as a growth strategy. The highest readiness was in technology (more than 74 percent), but they were just as bad at implementing the strategies. (Think you and your organization are ready? Information on and links to all my organization's free assessments can be found at the back of the book.)

This is a gap in leadership, and that should be good news. Because where there's a gap, there's an opportunity—in this case an opportunity to figure out how to drive inclusion throughout the organization. As leaders, our efforts so far have been on getting those diversity numbers up. But today that's just the minimum requirement for any organization. Simply achieving diversity will not give you a competitive advantage. You have to put that diversity to work. And that's where inclusion comes into play. We have to accept and *welcome* that productive tension I spoke about in Part 1 to break the cycle of exclusion that prevents the standardization of all "me's." The organizations that figure out how to do this will be the ones to achieve the biggest and most sustainable growth.

That's why a team with *diverse* experience will beat a team with *the same* experience almost every time, as long as the team is truly inclusive. As one leader said to me: "You have to purposefully engineer diversity when it comes to experience." That's what we need for inclusion and the standardization of "me."

When you have diversity, you have the foundation for innovation, but it's inclusion that unites individuals around a common goal they can all work differently to achieve. Inclusion lets individuals touch the business, influence more, help the organization mitigate risk, and neutralize uncertainty. In fact, employees and consumers often know what this requires better than the leaders and the organizations; they just don't have a platform to share and express their ideas and ideals.

Beyond Experience

Remember: The leaders who chose the diverse candidate in the scenario that opened this chapter did not just fail to look beyond diversity, they failed to look beyond experience. Inclusion demands that we look beyond experience and ask ourselves: Do you believe this person can do the job? If the answer is "Yes" and the person has the baseline experience needed, then ask yourself *What else do they bring?* Skills can be taught. In the case of the scenario, one candidate brought a face that looked familiar and the other brought a familiar face. Do you choose the one who looks like what you want, or the one you feel can do the best job?

Getting comfortable with capability rather than experience will ultimately result in more diverse hires overall. That opening scenario was designed to challenge your view that the only way to increase diversity is to force it. What you need to "force" here is your way of thinking. If you're only looking at applicants with elite education, and qualifications accessible only to those with certain backgrounds or particular training (that is, people who had access to the right opportunities), then your thinking is stuck in standardization and you are limiting your options from the start. If you learn to look beyond experience, then you start to truly open up your organization to bigger opportunities and new ways of thinking and hiring.

We can't afford to have organizations filled with people whose individual capacities are stifled in any way. Today our organizations are multigenerational, multicultural, multigender, and multitenure. With so many different mindsets and backgrounds, it's difficult to get everyone on the same page. Even people who check the same diversity boxes are not the same. I am Cuban American, but other Cuban Americans will not bring to their work the same experiences or capabilities that I bring to mine. We all fall into many groups and categories, and we bring our own mindsets to everything. So when leaders try to make their organizations "friendly" to these large, impersonal categories of people, all they really do is succeed in making people feel boxed in. Our individuality drives the need for inclusion. The winners are going to be the organizations that take this abundance of differences and find like-mindedness within it, and through inclusion allow differences to be their competitive advantage. They understand what's most important is the way we see and then respond to one another. That's why diversity will never lead to inclusion, why I want the word removed from the discussion. Diversity is not about being human. Diversity is as tribal as it gets. Inclusion is our way to reclaim our identities—the humanity that standardization stripped away.

Questions to Consider:
Inclusion

■ Do you/does your organization have a system for training leaders to identify individual capability when hiring, so that everyone can look beyond experience and education as the only indicators of potential and invite new thinking into the organization? Do you know how to identify individual capability, and give it at least equal weight?

■ Think of a time you/your organization fell into the standardization trap of diversity. If you saw it coming, did you avoid it? How did you deal—or not deal—with it?

■ Is it someone's job to make sure leaders have the knowledge, skills, and tools to make their departments more inclusive? Is someone accountable?

■ How are you/your leaders given training opportunities to learn how to be inclusive and forge relationships within departments and across the enterprise?

■ How is the Human Resources department positioned in your organization? How do you measure its contribution across the enterprise? Does it accelerate progress or slow it down?

PART 3

STANDARDIZATION:
TRIBAL
PERSONALIZATION:
HUMAN

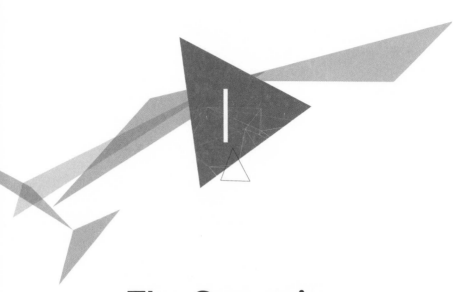

The Scenario

Your front-line employees have been burning the candle at both ends for weeks. You know the stress this puts on them physically and mentally, because you've been in their shoes. You make sure to let them know how grateful you are for their hard work and how much you appreciate all they're doing. But you can see them starting to fray, especially when one employee tells you he's "losing it." He asks for help to talk to a doctor his insurance does not cover and he cannot afford. Money is very tight, and there is no precedent for doing this. What do you do?

a. *Say no and make note of the meeting in the company files.* Alert HR. You can't afford this, and you need to document the problem so they can deal with it. Make sure you tell him you're sorry, how much you appreciate his hard work, and that you hope he works it out. He's a valuable member of the team.

b. *Talk to him yourself.* Talking doesn't cost anything. Plus, you've been in his shoes: Sharing your story is a way of honoring his telling you and offering support. HR would never approve anything else anyway. They're all about standardization, not personalization.

c. *Listen but don't act or react.* Not every problem is yours to solve, and it's not 100 percent clear this is a problem yet. Tell him you know how he is feeling, appreciate his letting you know, and assure him you will look into it if he can tough it out. But don't get involved emotionally.

d. *Gather the team for a bonding exercise to boost morale.* You saw how they were fraying. If this is happening to one person, it's probably happening to more of them. Work cannot be more important than their health and happiness as a team.

e. *Say yes and find a way to make it happen.* Tell him you know what this feels like by sharing your story. Ask him questions to find out more and how things might change. Forget about precedent—let this be the precedent. HR/the company will have to listen and then find a way to do it for others, too, to keep them healthy if you mean what you say about gratitude.

Choose your answer before proceeding.

Tribal (Us and Them) Versus Human (Us and Me)

Based on all we covered so far, you probably guessed answer *e* most reflects leadership in the age of personalization. You're correct. Let's break it down:

- Answer *a* is only about standardization. It makes the employee's story a compliance issue for HR. Sure, documentation is important, but at the complete expense of personalization and an inclusive workplace that truly cares? Words that seem to express caring (like *sorry* and *appreciate*) are as hollow as it gets in this answer.

■ Answer *b* is a step forward in so far as you've told your story, but it's all about you, not him. You share but don't ask any questions and listen to the answers. You simply talk *at* the person. That's standardizing the problem through your experience. It doesn't have anything to do with individuality or inclusion—or action.

■ Answer *c* steps into listening and individuality but at the expense of sharing—and there's no indication the employee's situation will influence a strategy for change. And telling him you know what he's feeling but showing no emotion makes the words as hollow as they were in answer *a*. He has no reason to trust you will do what you say.

■ Answer *d* lacks any individuality at all; it's all about the business, not the employees. This kind of forced bonding and manufactured fun may seem to be about inclusion, but they're really just about the *appearance* of inclusion. They have their time and place, but if not linked to a strategy for change, they don't solve anything.

■ Answer *e* has listening, sharing, and asking questions. It allows for the possibility of influence, and challenges HR to adapt and to adopt a new strategy for change that focuses on individual health and the health of the entire organization.

Answer *e* is where the leader landed in real life, though by his own admission it took longer than it should have to get there. In 2018, David McMillan, chef at the acclaimed Joe Beef in Montreal, told *Bon Appétit* magazine he realized he raised $750,000 a year to save the Atlantic salmon but didn't have $100 to give a staff member to talk to a therapist. This was all the more disturbing to McMillan, because the high-strung world of restaurants and fine dining had landed him in rehab for drinking that nearly cost him his livelihood and his life. Addiction to alcohol and drugs is common. McMillan knew firsthand the importance of being able to talk to someone: "The fact is, we're a motley crew of pirates who all need to speak to someone a bit. [We] raise so much money for things I honestly don't care about. Why don't we raise money for things we actually need and care about, right?"

McMillan shifted his mindset and started a nonprofit to have therapists talk to restaurant workers (not just his) and to send individuals to therapy or rehab. His story and actions are important and praiseworthy, but so is his kicking himself for taking so long to recognize the needs of his employees instead of the salmon. The pressure to do charity work is constant in his industry, and McMillan let that define what he cared about first: his status and reputation. He put thinking about fish over feeling for people—the opposite of what makes us human.

"We are not thinking machines that feel, we are feeling machines that think."

That's a quote from Thomas Damasio, a neuroscientist, and it exactly explains the difference between leadership in the age of standardization and leadership in the age of personalization. In the standardization mindset, we're actually working against our nature: We become thinking machines, conditioned to hide our emotions and personal feelings. When we do speak up individually—in big or small ways—like that employee in the scenario, we often get shut down and don't feel safe to do so again. Who among us has not felt beaten down by work and life—and hid that from the boss for fear of being judged, appearing weak, or getting fired?

In the age of personalization, we understand that our emotions and the feelings they produce rule our behavior and are what make us *human* beings. And their value is getting harder to deny. As I wrote this book, dozens of stories in major publications like *The Wall Street Journal*, *Inc.*, and *Fast Company* talked about companies looking for people who have what we often call "soft" skills. People who know the value of a handshake—one of the most important ways to establish trust between people. Who care about their relationships with their customers and can talk with others both casually and about matters of importance—not just focus on the transaction. Who can look at data and analytics from all sides and different perspectives—and be curious.

Most of us have been trained for the opposite of those things: "hard" skills that are specific, teachable, and measurable. Soft skills are more variable, especially those human skills that create feelings in others and draw them in. They are difficult to teach, control, automate, assimilate, and measure. Thus, they are misunderstood and oftentimes devalued.

But know this: Our feelings are powerful and hard to ignore. They can inspire us to collective and collaborative action that crosses all boundaries and allows us to let go of the status quo—or they can make us hold on tighter. Emotions can also be manipulated to divide us as much as they unite us. It's not news to say that politicians, pundits, and anyone else who sways our emotions can manipulate our feelings and thus dictate our actions and beliefs. On the one hand, it's nice to feel inspired by leaders who make us feel good about who we are and what we're doing. On the other hand, when those leaders make us feel that others are the source of our problems and threaten our safety, status, beliefs, and identities, this becomes a problem. When that happens, instead of accepting responsibility in whole or in part for our circumstances and actions, or allowing for different perspectives, we unite with others who share the same points of view and reject, blame, and/or attack others.

We call this *tribal behavior* or *tribalism*: the exclusion of—and often contempt for—others who do not conform to the tribe and the way "we" identify. And if you think that sounds a lot like leadership in the age of standardization, in which the business, its brand, and mission define the individual, you're right.

The Standardization of "Us" Is
Tribal Thinking and Feeling

Today's political landscape and America itself seem to be locked in a fierce tribalism of identity politics, in a search to reinforce or reclaim status that comes from a scarcity mindset (nothing is ever enough, so for me to win, you have to lose). This has perpetuated a rush to take sides, judge each other, and intentionally to provoke blame and hatred, things at the very core of treating others as less than human. Business leaders can and must act differently, even if our politicians cannot. Leaders can have an abundance mindset that is win-win for all. But not if they remain siloed and status driven.

Tribal thinking and the silos it creates are based on status quo and exclusion ("us" *versus* "them") rather than individuality and inclusion ("me" *and* "us"). Tribal thinking and silos in business put people into the boxes they check (much like diversity) and divide departments, work, people, identities, and our stories from each other. This makes the people in the silos less cross-functional, collaborative, and communicative with each other—less *human* toward each other— just as it does in the highly polarized and contentious world we live in. Organizations then reinforce those silos through forced assimilation to

- job titles and descriptions that stifle individual identities
- metrics that encourage results over methods and discourage cross-functionality and collaboration that lead to inclusion
- data and digital transformations that strive for efficiencies and automation to the exclusion of individuality.

Most organizations are designed to perform this way—as tribes, the members surrounded by people they like and who are like them. This tribalism gives them license to care more about surrounding themselves with people who conform to what they think and believe, and to exclude, erase, or minimize anyone who doesn't. This results in relationships only with those who agree with them or reaffirm their opinions (confirmation bias) and teams and organizations that lack productive tension, because they do not listen to learn and uncover new opportunities.

Finding "your people" can be a good thing. I understand the impulse for people to find the influence they've been denied by uniting around an identity, whether internally (through an employee resource group) or externally (founding an all-woman tech firm, an all-black dance troupe, or an all-Hispanic investment firm). But that doesn't mean they are immune to the mistakes of tribal thinking or that their efforts lead to inclusion. They've just removed one factor. They can still lack inclusivity and create the tribal behavior that undermines leadership in the age of personalization—no matter how strong or well-meaning an initiative is. The question for them and for all of us is: *Where do the tribal lines stop being drawn and the human connections to all people start again? When do we stop making others check boxes?*

Tribal thinking tends to get smaller and smaller—sometimes right down to a single issue that is so important we discount anything about it that bothers us. We see this in politics all the time: People vote for candidates whose position on a polarizing issue aligns with theirs and ignore broader character or even criminal issues. People are willing to believe the worst stories about a candidate on the other side—often through negative stories that have no foundation in fact—because that person does not conform to their norm. We also see this with customers and brands in business. According to a Cone Communications CSR Study, 78 percent of Americans want companies to address important social justice issues, and 87 percent will purchase a product because a company advocates for an issue they care about. But does that mean you should only patronize brands that share your values, regardless of what they sell? Should gun rights advocates who love tents boycott Dick's Sporting Goods because the chain pulled guns from some store shelves? Should

LGBTQ people who love a chicken sandwich boycott Chick-fil-A because of the company's stance on gay marriage? Should women not watch CBS after hearing about allegations against Les Moonves?

I can't answer that. What I can ask is: *Whose values are you living: yours as an individual, or yours as defined by your tribe?* And how are you seeing and treating those on the other side, or who work for the brands that don't represent your values? Sure, a boycott can impact the bottom line, but what about a relationship that might change minds stuck on the other side of the story?

I'll repeat it one more time: *Where do we stop drawing that tribal line?* When do we stop putting ourselves in boxes and causing unproductive tension like the "wrong" answers to the scenario that opened Part 1 and this chapter?

How do we pull ourselves out of this standardization trap and let go?

The Standardization of Me Is Human Feeling and Thinking

As human beings, it's natural for us to surround ourselves with people like ourselves. This is especially true in business when members of a team (that is, tribe) have been together for a long time. They know each other's habits, strengths, and quirks. They're used to each other. They *like* each other. Teams like that, when having to make a new hire, often use words like "she's not a good fit for our team" or "he doesn't suit the culture of the organization" as reasons for not hiring someone. Those *sound* positive but too often they're excuses. What they're really saying is "that person threatens my status" or "that's not the way we do things and I don't want to change." That's stagnation. That's holding back the team and the organization from the benefits of new thinking and from the expertise of someone new, smart, capable, and knowledgeable about the market. That's *limiting*.

Now imagine that a team finds a person who fits the job requirements perfectly, and knows he can do the job, but he's also . . . "prickly." He has strong opinions about the team's approach to its customers and about the leader's plan. He has serious questions about its viability and whether it will lead to the results the team expects. The team is uncomfortable with his questions *and* his personality. Most leaders tell me in that situation they would hire someone else. Sure, they acknowledge the prickly person's expertise, but his contrarian attitude and his personality make them think he will just slow things down, be hard to work with, and destroy the team dynamic. He might make them rethink their plans. He's questioning the conclusions the team and the organization have already reached. And that's . . . a *bad* thing? Is it really the prickly personality that makes them uncomfortable, or is it that the person makes them think about things they're not thinking about? Is it really about fit or is that an excuse for taking the easy way out and maintaining the status quo—the operative and tribal word being *status*?

As soon as someone starts talking about status and norms when dismissing a person or idea, you've found your constructive interruption for challenging the status quo. You've found contrarian views that could offer valuable perspective and strengthen your ultimate plan. You just have to be human enough to welcome those views. If you throw people out every time they become inconvenient, make you uncomfortable, or have personality or point of view conflicts, then you're not only undermining inclusion and thus personalization, but also reinforcing tribal behavior to maintain that status quo.

Leadership in the age of personalization requires the exact opposite approach: Assume positive intent, refuse to whitewash differences that are part of individual identities, and unite the goals of the organization around those identities. That's what the standardization of me is all about: standardizing a way that allows us to be less selfish and more human. Help your people discover what they have in common, and *then* their differences. When they do that, they have more than a connection to each other—they have intimacy, all because the organization brought them together. It's not too hard to see how these humans can then unite around their success and goals and those of the organization and their leaders, to maximize everyone's potential. You have standardized "me" while reinforcing feelings of "us." Throughout the organization

- leaders exude confidence in themselves and admit that other people have valuable perspectives and great ideas;
- the silos that got in the way of working together are gone without minimization of individual differences;
- real relationships have formed, built on mutual respect and trust, no matter the hierarchy or rank.

Personalization is about our human side. About respect, not recognition. Standardization assumes the individual would, should, and must conform to a tribal standard. This tug of war between tribal and human is the last gasp of leadership in the age of standardization. The only way to win that war is to stop fighting. Stop playing the game on standardization's terms and let go of the rope. **Cultures won't change unless we interrupt the limitations of tribal thinking—and get past it.**

A human approach to leadership shakes us from our selfish silos and makes us want to seek and have relationships based on genuine feelings and emotions that lead to caring, understanding, and inclusion. This requires us to truly know our customers and employees, by finding out who they are by listening to their stories. When we do, we have an intimacy that compels our "better human" to emerge—one that can have a direct impact on individual performance for everyone.

Because human thinking is holistic thinking.

Who Are We Solving For: Ourselves or Others?

I f there is one word that polarizes leaders and forces them into tribal positions almost immediately when I say it, it has to be *Millennials*. Millennials are *soooooo* annoying, right? That's certainly the story many of us have been told and are stuck in about the most scrutinized and analyzed generation to ever enter the workforce. I couldn't possibly count the number of times I've heard all Millennials disparaged universally by leaders and talking heads and in blog posts and articles. I get that there have always been tensions between the generations, but what is it about Millennials that has raised such ire and forces us to retreat so far into tribal behavior?

- *Is it that they're always looking for meaning in what they do and the companies they work for?* It isn't just them: According to a *Harvard Business Review* study, 90 percent of Americans would take a pay cut for a more meaningful job.
- *Is it their lack of loyalty?* Most studies do show around half of Millennials plan to leave their jobs after two years and a super-majority will leave by five. Yet a Bridge study shows that 90 percent of Millennials want to grow their careers with their current companies. So why aren't they getting what they need to stay?
- *Is it their seeming sense of entitlement in wanting to be included in all decisions, and advance quicker than previous generations ever did?* Maybe they just want to be engaged and are looking for more to do? According to HR Drive, only 29 percent of Millennials are engaged at work, 16 percent are actively disengaged, and 55 percent are not engaged at all.

I could keep going. For every solid statistic and argument, I could find an equally solid statistic and argument that counters or contextualizes it. But the last one—given the size of the Millennial population and its disengagement—should awaken the need for change even in those stuck in a standardization mindset: Gallup calculated that a disengaged employee costs $3,400 for every $10,000 of salary.

As one senior leader told me, she sees the battle between standardization and personalization as the battle between corporate America and Millennials and, soon, Gen Z. Are we going to dismiss that? They are the leaders of the future, with growing spending power. They can teach us much more than just how to maximize our social media or fix our computers (though they are good at that). Why wouldn't we want them to influence our businesses? Why wouldn't anyone want to tap into the brains of younger professionals who will be shaping the future of businesses—as consumers, employees, and leaders? Why wouldn't we want to face the productive tension and emotions that come with it, and use them to energize and motivate us— to maximize everyone's potential? Yes, our first steps toward executing this will be flawed. There's no shame in that. Real change is never clean or easy, free of anger or controversy.

I know, because I went through it myself.

The Millennial and Me

When I met Guilherme, he had all the skills I wanted in an employee. He was shy and lacking confidence but also ambitious and looking for experience. I saw potential and then . . . I got a little annoyed. The more he opened up and understood my business, he started to talk about things that I disagreed with. I appreciated his perspectives, but he was challenging the way I had done things in the past. His suggestions annoyed me.

But then I turned the spotlight on myself and asked: Why was I creating an adversarial relationship? Guilherme was the same great "kid" I'd hired months before and learning how things worked at my company. Was he questioning me to undermine my leadership or just questioning to understand? Did I see him as entitled because his limited experience diminished my decades of hard-fought experience? I expected him to work for the goals of the company, but did I really want someone who did things the way I had always done them? Or did I want someone to see and seize new opportunities?

I didn't use these exact words, but I realized I was not leading with a personalization mindset, and that I was being tribal in my thinking. I was expecting Guilherme to see what I was seeing, not because I wanted him to but because that's how I saw things. I always wanted his diversity of thought, but by treating him as a human and learning to open myself up, I allowed him to influence more quickly. I let go, and when I did I began to realize why the way I was approaching the business didn't work as well as I expected it to. Even though I had started the company, created all the content, and determined how it should be marketed and delivered, I was wrong. I'm in the business of serving the needs of others and managing change for organizations filled with people too afraid or too exhausted and unprepared to deal with those changes. But the only people who understood my approach were the most senior people, and that limited my reach. That was my fault—because I was speaking in a way that appealed to the senior leaders and no one else.

Guilherme reshaped my thinking and retaught me. He showed me that if only senior people understood the services my organization was offering, it was a slow death for my business. I had to bring it down several octaves in vocabulary and enthusiasm. To get to the larger audience, I had to change how I presented my work, learn how to provide enough context, and then say things in as few words as possible to get to the point.

The important thing is Guilherme's and my interactions today are not tribal but human—that we make it safe to be human with each other and have a real relationship. When I resolved to learn from Guilherme, I became more confident in him and pushed him to keep seeing these things that I didn't. As a result, he became more confident in his work. Today, he influences how I think. I don't present him strategies to execute or for feedback; we collaborate on them. I use his perspectives to test mine by considering how those perspectives might connect differently with others. He has opened my mind to be more inclusive, and as a result, I am exposed to perspectives that ensure I stay well ahead of the trends in my work. He challenges me when I am acting inauthentically and sweating the smallest details. When he doesn't understand a decision I've made, I take the time to explain it to him. When things don't move as quickly as he would like, I help him ask questions as to why. Even if I end up rejecting Guilherme's ideas (or when he rejects mine) or when compromise is not possible, we have increased our respect for each other.

Ask yourself about your organization and leadership: *Which stories are you telling and listening to, ones that open you up or shut you down?* Shutting down is certainly easier; the status quo fights back hard in your mind as you try to let go of the story of the past. After all, that story has been repeating itself for generations now. You must put practices in place to break down the silos and get people to experience each other's stories. So how do leaders and organizations start executing this with an age of personalization mindset and learn these stories from their people and customers to build a future founded on leadership in the age of personalization? By talking *with* each other—not *at* each other.

Let Go of the Past

If we all know the value of one-on-one, face-to-face conversations, why aren't we having them? Well . . . sometimes we *think* we are. In the past few years organizations have focused on helping their people have "courageous conversations"—a term synonymous with being open and willing to learn from each other, resolve relational conflicts, and/or having open dialogues. The goals of these conversations are wisdom, understanding, and trust. Sounds admirable. I used to think so, too. But today I see none of that is possible while leading with a standardization mindset. Most courageous conversations I have witnessed have been artificial, forced efforts at inclusion. Why? Because they start by defining talking with each other as a courageous feat instead of a human one. Because of diversity, we think it requires courage to propel a human conversation, when really all it propels is more fear and tribalism. Do you think people really tell the truth about anything when they feel this way? The problem is most leaders don't see the importance of allowing their people the space to feel safe to speak up. Prioritizing these human conversations shifts the mindset to the standardization of "me," to listening to learn. To asking questions. To showing respect. To allowing others to influence us. To seeing the value of other methods, strategies, and approaches—even if we choose a different path.

To get there from here, organizations must stop controlling the individual and finally allow individual employees and customers to guide the organization's growth strategies. And it is what your people expect, especially those Millennials who are often called the "inclusion generation." But don't do it for "them." Do it for everyone and *with* everyone as individuals—as humans—and create cultures based on real relationships filled with people who find purpose and like-mindedness within their differences. Who feel they belong as part of a healthy whole, have common values and beliefs, cultivate trust and engagement, and grow and evolve together through their individual impact and influence.

Sounds great, right? Easier said than done.

It takes wisdom, trust, and courage to let someone influence us, especially someone younger. Like any change, it's uncomfortable, because it challenges the very nature and value of our experience. But that's the point. I don't need or want another me and I don't need or want Guilherme to go through what I did to get to where I am. I want to help him find his own path while achieving the goals of our company. It's invigorating, not annoying. Sure, I want him to deliver the best for our clients and me, but I would prefer he exceed expectations any way he wants, not comply with what I have done before to the exact terms I've used.

Leaders: let go of the expression "That's not how we did it in the past." That line is just a veiled excuse for tribal behavior when our experience and status is threatened. For most of us, if we reapplied for the jobs we have, we wouldn't qualify for them in the age of personalization. It's time that we all learn to requalify ourselves as humans for the jobs we're in and rethink what jobs we really should be in. Fail to do that and your Millennials and soon Gen Z's will move on, and the statistics about job hopping will become a self-fulfilling prophecy. They are not going to go through what their leaders went through, waiting for annual or even semiannual reviews and "paying their dues" with time served. They are not going to follow their parents into that time trap. They are going to leave. They are done. Better to assume the best and allow them to push you to consider the possibilities and opportunities—and not wait years for you to understand this as your first bosses did.

Think of it this way: Would you make a client or customer wait three months for a product or service that takes two weeks to produce simply because it took three months a generation ago? Of course not. Then why make your people do that when time is so much more compressed today when it comes to learning skills and gaining experience? Break free from the mindset of standardization where standardization is about status quo. Shift that tribal mindset of the past to a human one for the future.

IV

Data Geeks Versus
Human Geeks

A friend who is a senior executive working with people analytics was the one who told me the quote I used earlier: "We are not thinking machines that feel, we are feeling machines that think." I couldn't agree more. In an age when we have algorithms capable of telling us what we want, need, and will like, and AI becoming more and more "personalized" every day, it can seem technology is leading with personalization. But what it has really given us is the illusion that everything is more personal, because we can customize our cars, our homes, our phones, our refrigerators . . . We call them "smart devices," but who is the smart one? In many respects, technology is really just personalizing standardization to help organizations make more money by tethering us to their devices.

We need to balance the need for technology with the standardization of me—use its efficiencies to get back more of the time for human conversations that standardization stripped us of. **We don't need more data geeks. We need more human geeks.**

Sure, digital transformations and Big Data make it seem that we need actual humans less than ever. And in some ways, that is true: If a skill can become automated, then a human can be replaced. Initially, organizations needed a lot of people who were technical experts in those areas to set up the infrastructure, software, programming, and more. But once those things are established, organizations don't need more people to gather data or put things together. The jobs that they needed ten people to do five years ago need three people now. The other seven people who do only those tasks are obsolete—unless they have skills that cannot be replaced by the very technology they helped enable or by cheaper labor abroad who learned to do what they do. That's why human geeks are the most valuable people these days—the ones who can translate data into something other humans who lack their technological training can understand and use. We need humans who can look at the data and ask questions from different perspectives.

- What is it telling us—now and long term?
- How does it look if you look from other vantage points? What does it look like from the sales and marketing side? Accounting? Inventory? IT? Manufacturing? Distribution? Logistics?
- What does it look like from the employee side?

Take the 21st-century field of people analytics (sometimes called HR analytics). It uses data to help leaders make decisions about their customers and employees, but many leaders have no idea what people analytics means, let alone what it does. The same friend who gave me that quote told me that one of the fastest growing practices in people analytics is solving for business needs—using data to accelerate collaboration between existing teams and new hires, merged teams resulting from acquisitions or consolidation, and global teams that must navigate complex conditions. The challenge isn't that these organizations lack data. It's that they don't have the human ability to turn the data into a story that helps forge a new culture and way of working centered on personalization.

Yes, I said "story." We need the human geek storytellers as much as, if not more than, the data geek scientists. We need people who can connect the dots and can ask, answer, and anticipate questions from all angles and can present them in ways that you don't need a PhD in statistics to follow. You can't automate those skills—at least not yet. After all, it's not like the data we get is completely objective. Users of Big Data have discovered the AI they thought would be free from bias (because numbers never lie, right?) actually reflects the biases of the humans doing the programming and feeding in the data. In other words, AI was *tribal.*

Of course, Big Data, AI, and digital transformations are the future and we need the good standardized information they give us. But that should allow us more time to share our stories and build relationships that transform our mindset and open us up, instead of shutting us down to each other. You can have all the infrastructure you need to support the digital transformation. You can have AI and algorithms that support all that. But who pulls the story together? Humans. Who is going to see different conclusions for different circumstances and weigh the information? Humans. You still need humans to guide the context and ask where the story could go and make recommendations. In 2018, Elon Musk replaced robots on the Tesla Model 3 assembly line with humans because the humans were more adaptable to problems and changes. The democratization of data requires the same thing. Fail to do this and too much standardization will further strip away our humanity and enable the tribalization of data.

Personalization compels us to see each other not as a number, not defined by how we look, how much we make, or how we vote or feel about a certain issue, but as an individual. This is the essence of what humanity represents. Let's take the time to get to know each other as individuals. Let's be human again.

Questions to Consider:
Human

- Have you/your organization taken the time to brainstorm and write down the thinking and habits that must be constructively interrupted in order to be more inclusive as a team?

- How have teams, departments, and the organization as a whole defined "a good fit" in the past? Is there anything about that definition that needs to be rethought in order to be more inclusive?

- How does your organization actively engage with the variety of groups representing the shifting demographics in the markets it serves? Are they seen as cost centers? Through the lens of reputation management tribes? Or as measurable contributors to the organization's growth strategies?

- How do you let all people influence your thinking— especially if you don't agree with them? Name one time someone made you rethink your approach to something simply because you sat down and talked with each other?

- How are you listening to the stories your employees, customers, and data are telling you?

Stuck in Standardization

Diversity programs put people in boxes, so
we cling to our tribes and labels and
see each other as other.

Leadership in the
Age of Personalization

When we turn diversity into inclusion,
we stop being tribal and start seeing
each other as human.

PART 4

STANDARDIZATION:
BRAND IDENTITY
PERSONALIZATION:
INDIVIDUAL IDENTITIES

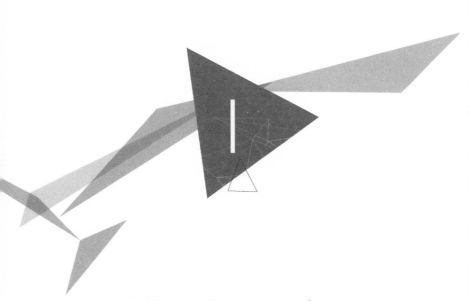

The Scenario

One of your oldest customers—someone you consider a friend—fires you after twenty years. He says he "doesn't know you anymore." You think you know why. You used to do business face-to-face and with a handshake. Now it's all emails and texts from your team to his. Phone calls go unreturned. Messages too often are ignored. When the customer needs to speak to someone, it's never a conversation with a real relationship behind it. Even when there's a problem, it's always "I'll get back to you later," usually with another email. No conversation, listening, or broader awareness of the issue. What do you decide to do?

a. *Let this client go.* Sometimes letting go is the best thing for everyone. It's hard to lose employees or customers that have been with you for so long, but this one is stuck in the past and can be more trouble than he's worth. The world is full of business to replace anyone. Call the customer back and say you understand.

b. *Send out a company-wide email.* Report what happened and remind your people that an essential part of the company's mission is to "treat customers like family." Ask your team to get together and email strategies for better customer service that you will review in the individual and group meetings your assistant will schedule as soon as possible. In the meantime, tell everyone you expect them to connect with their customers and begin regular conversations with them.

c. *Gather the team and let them have it.* "We had to hear that from a customer of twenty years!? Has anyone even read our mission statement? We need to come together as a team and make sure this never happens again. Call all your customers *now* and check in. There will be serious consequences if we lose any others."

d. *Gather the team and let them hear the story of what happened.* Without yelling, make sure everyone knows things have to change. Send the entire team out immediately for face-to-face chats with every customer, no matter how much time it takes or how many hundreds of locations there are. Book your trip to visit that friend who fired you.

Choose your answer carefully before proceeding.

II

What Are You Solving For: The Brand or the Individual?

T he answer most people choose is *d*. Answer *d* and the set-up for the scenario are also basically the script from a 1990 United Airlines commercial. Search for "1990 United Airlines Commercial Speech" and watch it now to refresh your memory, or if you haven't seen it, don't remember it, or weren't born when it aired. It's powerful, no matter how you feel about United. While the communication methods the leader refers to in the actual commercial are phone calls and faxes (Google it, Gen Z!) and the actors who make up the leadership team he speaks to are overwhelmingly male and white (which no commercial would dare show today), the ad feels as real as any scenario I could have created from the news or my experiences. Which is why I have seen it used in leadership trainings decades later.

But does that mean *d* is the "right" answer? No, and not just because the commercial predates TSA checks and the global economy of the 21st century that would make this leader's solution a time, cost, and logistical nightmare today. It's because the action of the leader in the ad (and answer *d*), while a feel-good, big, and bold action, does *not* demonstrate leadership in the age of personalization. It's quite literally a commercial about standardization. It may have connected in 1990 as a demonstration of exemplary team leadership, but today, I wonder how many of those people in the room would feel the same way.

In fact, taken at face value, answer *d* is no less standardized an answer than *c*. The leader's action may seem proactive, personalized, and much nicer in *d*, but it's still standardization. It also shows why it is so hard to execute leadership in the age of personalization when it comes to allowing individual identities to influence the brand: because the kinder, gentler side of standardization makes us think we already do.

Standardization with a Smile

Let me start by reinforcing something I said earlier: Regular, sustained, authentic one-on-one and face-to-face communication (that is, leading in person)—talking with each other not at each other—is essential to *any* successful leadership style, not just leadership in the age of personalization. It's the foundation for our closest relationships in business and in life. It makes others feel important and allows us to do more than simply read or hear their words. We can see the whole person, feel their feelings, read their body language and facial expressions. We can ask questions, they can ask questions, and we can see if they are actually listening to our answers.

But doing these things successfully requires practice, commitment, and a mindset that they matter. Do the leader and organization in the scenario really seem able to do that, based on the description of how they're doing business? What would it even mean to the customers? What does it mean to the team in the room? Has he really learned from his mistakes? This is a leader who wants his employees to go out and shake hands with their customers to establish trust and connection, but has he extended that handshake to his team? And what about leaving room for customers who actually prefer email over a handshake?

Yelling at people or calmly telling them a story—both deliver a face-to-face moment, but neither is necessarily an individualized or inclusive one. The leader's actions in answer *d* show some vulnerability and are obviously more civil and less morale-destroying than answer *c,* but they neither consider the relationships between the other customers and his employees (that is, their individuality) nor allow the employees to influence a strategy for change (inclusion). In answers *c* and *d,* his face-to-face meeting only reinforces his will to affirm his decision and have his people do what they're told. This expectation for compliance, which used to work in the age of standardization, is not always mean or Big Brother–like. Sometimes it comes candy-coated.

Answer *d* viewed through the lens of personalization is personalizing a strategy for the *brand's identity*, not a new strategy for letting the individual identities of the team members and the customers define the business. Because he is profoundly human, the leader *seems* to be leading with personalization. But if someone in his position thought he was doing that today, he would be acting—which is what most leaders and organizations do every day: They *act* like—and may even *think* that—they are genuinely embracing individuality and inclusion and allowing their people influence. But they aren't.

Even answer *a*, which ignores the problem and is one big rationalization for not changing, is more individualized than *d*. At least it considers (in a small way) why the relationship between the leader and the customer failed, doesn't project that failure on the entire organization, or demand change by throwing money at the problem. The only answer that in any way considers both inclusion and individuality is *b*. Yes, it's flawed: Emailing the news is more impersonal than face-to-face; the leader shows no vulnerability; and he makes no specific promises on when or how the individual responses will be reviewed. But at least it steps into a mindset that isn't "my way or the highway," so to speak.

A true strategy for leadership in the age of personalization might begin with the scenario as described, but then the leader explains what he is doing to try to make it right, and asks employees for feedback. Then he allows the individuals to define and influence the way forward and decode what their customers need, in order to achieve the same goals as their leader. Their leader's wisdom would allow them to discover what they still need to know to influence their own way. He would value the best parts of everyone's identity and their capacity and capability to solve for things in the future. For example, the leader could still mandate teams connect with customers, but would listen to how they are doing that and find their own paths to greater intimacy and deeper relationships with them. He could help teams rehearse their own conversations with their customers, offer feedback after they happen, and then offer trips to see them if needed. The leader would then ask the team, as he did in answer *b*, how each individual can use their identity to influence the leader's and the organization's strategy for change.

And if he had made all that a priority, as well as having regular one-on-one meetings with his team and that customer, he likely never would have been in this situation to begin with. (But then there would be no moving commercial.) That may be why so many people today say *d* feels like the right answer: It *is* moving. And it's easy to execute. It sells a kinder, gentler version of the command-and-control leadership style that defined the age of standardization for more than a century.

There Is No *I* in Model T

When Henry Ford first started producing cars at the turn of the 20th century, workers built whole cars themselves—a highly inefficient process that made those cars expensive. Ford needed mass production, not artisanal production, to make the Model T more than a luxury. Enter the assembly line. The idea wasn't new but Ford executed it on a scale and with a degree of efficiency previously unheard of. Individual workers were retrained to work together to perform specific sequential tasks in the building process, rather than all of them. This required hiring more workers to assemble a car, but Ford believed the increase in production would more than pay for the increased labor costs *and* allow him to reduce the price of the Model T. He was right. Out of the gate, Ford's assembly line produced a car almost 80 percent faster than a single worker. Plus, production was continuous. If one person was out, another could learn the task quickly and step in.

But there was one problem: His current workers hated the change. They were upset by the line's repetitive work and lack of ownership. Many of them quit. Even an increase in wages went only so far to retain them. Ford realized he needed to do more than control the way cars were manufactured: He needed to control the workers who manufactured them. So he created a "sociological department" and made every current worker and applicant submit to its evaluation. The department even visited homes to ensure workers met certain criteria deemed essential for assembly line success, like being thrifty, not drinkers, not living in sin, and willing to take only standard Christian holidays. Those who passed the "test" were promised double the industry standard wages.

Ford's ensuing ability to retain his workers and increase their productivity resulted in even greater production, and indeed, those workers could afford the cars they were building. He was so proud of his success he shared it, welcoming competitors, executives from other countries, politicians to see what he had done. He thought standardization of work and workers was the path to American greatness and influence. He wanted it to reshape American manufacturing, the American workplace, and the workforce in general. Thus the age of standardization was born.

Henry Ford not only standardized work, but also standardized workers who had to be willing, able, and required to give up their individuality and identity to the brand. There was no individuality on the assembly line, and no *identities* but the Ford brand. This was the definition of the great American melting pot, only in business practices: Strip away individual identity and assimilate the individuals to the brand. In return, the brand would define their identity. Allow that loss of identity, conform, and work hard, and those individuals could realize the American dream of opportunity, freedom, and equality for themselves and their children. Buy a car. Buy a home. Raise a family.

By almost every measure, my family lived this dream. My parents immigrated to America in the 1960s, and my father built a successful career in corporate America. He was a chemist and an integral part of the quality control team that formulated an iconic American brand: Miller Lite. My parents bought a house, raised a family, and loved their new country. So why did my father want me to think differently when I graduated college in the 1980s and took my first corporate job at a well-known and successful wine and spirits company?

My father could hear the struggle in my voice. That company had the classic top-down, best-practice, fear-based culture common in the age of standardization. I was told I had to deliver results or I would be out in thirty days. I was given the company playbook and told to follow it. Individuality? Communication? Nope: The only things that mattered were the transaction and compliance. Our relationships were defined by the company: A group of high performers who respected the standards—but who also didn't believe in them. Just like at Ford, this standardized process produced results that padded our paychecks, so we also didn't question them. Not that they all needed questioning. I know that standards I learned at that job—attention to detail, daily reporting that elevated my sense of accountability and responsibility, and teamwork—have been critical to my success. In fact, I learned to appreciate the power of methodologies. But it was never about *me*, or rather the standardization of me: my individuality, the different opportunities I saw for the brand, or what I wanted for my future. There was no balance between standardization and personalization. It was about the brand controlling us: Do what you're told, and you will do great here. If I followed the rules, I would be rewarded with a salary and benefits that would allow me to live the same dream my parents had.

But soon it bothered me the same way it had bothered the workers at Ford decades before. So my father had made sure I knew one thing the company didn't: how special I was as an individual. He wanted me to hold onto my individuality, not let go of it. He was determined that I never lose myself to an organization that demanded I do that. He wanted me to hold onto my story and my individual identity—to know I was defined by what I did well, not by my job title or what my employer wanted. He prepared me to be who I was in a world in which the Holy Grail for brands was to script our feelings into commercials like that one for United that move us to fly the friendly skies, reach out and touch someone, or have a Coke and a smile. Those ads and that scripting bend consumers and employees to the brand's will. Inside the office they did the same thing, stripping away that individuality. If I let go of who I was, then I would never be able to authentically lead and help others find and hold onto their identities—and influence change in those organizations.

I held on.

I believe now that my father saw something more than just his kid struggling to come to grips with the working world. He saw that the climate was changing—that more people like me would start to push back in a way he never could. That we push back even against nice leaders like the one in the scenario. If leaders fail to shift their mindset and listen to and learn from the stories of others, beyond their own—if they refuse to let go and allow their employees and customers to influence how the story of the organization is written—then they will lose more of those customers *and* employees (who will nicely quit the brand) and fail to grow. Their approach will fail for the same reason their diversity programs fail to result in sustainable levels of inclusion that drive growth. *Because their organizations are not committed to embracing differences as opportunities; instead they continue to strip employees of their identities and make them assimilate to the needs of the organization.*

There's More Than One *I* in "Identities"

"I need to know who I am. I know what I stand for. I know I want purpose and meaning in my work. But I don't know who I am. That's what keeps me up at night." Too many leaders and employees have said some version of that to me. What they are all saying is, *"I don't know my identity. No one knows me as an individual."*

This is heartbreaking to me: The one person you must know in your life is yourself. When the pressure is on and you are forced to make life-defining decisions, the ability to know yourself is tested.

- Do you know yourself enough?
- Have you lived a life that allows you to know yourself enough?
- Have you broken free from what others think your life path should be?

These are exactly the questions that keep those leaders and employees awake at night. This is the tension they feel: Restricted and limited throughout their lives, they have tried to break away from standardization yet have been defined and crushed by it. Most of them thus feel comfortable living in the age of standardization—and unprepared to lead. Yet they want to feel and be significant, not just successful. Today we've entered a new Age of Personalization, in which employees and consumers want to align with brands that are capable of leading and serving them based on the person's own values, unique needs, and desires. This shifts the balance of power from brands and businesses to individuals—to the standardization of "me." Organizations that make employees and consumers feel included and understood on an individual level will have a huge advantage over those that don't.

Of course, it may seem that organizations are already doing that: Unlike when I started in business, today's employees have evolved to have a much deeper sense of their own selves at work, where personality tests are common (for example, StrengthsFinder, Myers-Briggs, DISC). Organizations are filled with people who have learned at least some basics about their personalities, strengths and weaknesses, and work styles. Similarly, there are competency measurements and assessments that help leaders and organizations understand us as people and help us understand who we are. But are those same organizations providing ways for individuals to actually *use* that self-knowledge and be self-directed? If not, what a waste. **The age of personalization is about individuals being self-directed and ensuring the success and significance of the organization they serve.** Without that, all that knowledge just becomes a means to one end: standardization—putting people in boxes. It's a slippery slope back into tribal, not human.

Consider this: If you had a team of five people working on a major redesign of your systems and customer service, would you want five individuals who think like the brand working together to create the strategy? Or would you want five individuals who think for themselves on behalf of the brand, working through the tension and aligning what they think with what the brand represents, to create the strategy? I'm hoping you choose the latter. That's what you get in personalization when you have people with strong, secure, and credible identities. Each individual identity brings to the team a unique blend of thinking, expertise, and experience that gives them distinction, skills, and interests that make them particularly suited to solve certain problems.

But allowing individual identities to define the brand identity takes a concerted, strategic effort that many organizations are not investing in. They still see individuality as something to be eliminated and assimilated. When there was one brand, one identity, one way of doing things, standardization—like the Ford assembly line—succeeded in defining the identity of individual employees and customers. When customers bought in the age of standardization, they wanted the promise (and status) of what the brand's products or services offered, not something customizable. When employees entered offices in the age of standardization, they were told that if they did these five things (whatever they might be), the probability of generating those ten outcomes (whatever they were) was high. Multiply this thinking across the department, and then departments across the enterprise, and the results came in, just like they did in my first job. During those times, we actually saw the value of standardization, because we saw the results and felt like we were contributing to the success of the organization. But what we didn't realize is that we were widgets generating outcomes. We were being trained and prepared to be limited—and highly dependent on the business for our success and happiness.

The age of personalization came first in the marketplace as customers demanded and expected more customization from their products and services. As a result, most organizations today understand more and more the importance of individuality, rather than the transaction, to define their products, serve their customers, and increase customer lifetime value—even if that understanding has been slower to come when it relates to customer service. I'm not just talking about the seeming impossibility of getting a person on the phone when you have a problem, but any interaction that requires asking questions of people and listening to the answers. For example, health care providers have spent decades building business models focused on increasing volume—a fee-for-service model. The result is a system that treats a 24-year-old diagnosed with breast cancer the same way it would treat a 50-year-old with the same diagnosis. Sure, procedures need to be standardized to preserve quality of care, but certainly a 24-year-old's life decisions will be driven by different perspectives than someone middle-aged. The system is built in a way that makes it hard for institutions to see—and treat—people as individuals. No matter how much a doctor or nurse may care for patients as the unique people they are, that same doctor or nurse (and all care providers) still has to function within a system built around billing codes and line items and volume. But the industry is trying to change by shifting its mindset to value-based health care. The goal is to improve the health of its shifting populations and to provide a better experience for patients and communities, while still managing costs. It's an enormous challenge.

The challenges presented by individuality are even bigger when it comes to seeing and serving employees as unique individuals and designing systems to make sure those individuals are included at every level. Most organizations think individuals are hierarchy driven—like in the age of standardization—but they're not; they're capacity driven. If more leaders and organizations understood this, they could create real strategies for change and grow much faster than they ever have before. If they saw capacity and capability as equally if not more important than experience alone. If they saw the benefit in having a brand identity influenced by different *identities*. But they've been taught something different.

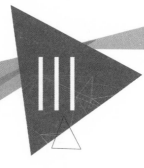

The Standardization of "Me" Versus "Me's"

"Put your coat on, I'm cold." That's what a friend of mine heard a mother say to her child as they left a store one Chicago night. That simple turn of phrase perfectly sums up how our individuality gets stripped away. I believe something, so you must, too. I think something, so you must, too. I feel something, so you must, too. The organization and brand work this way, so you must, too.

Too many leaders have "grown up" being standardized this way (that is, being told to put on their coat because the organization is cold) and can't see any other way now but to comply. They didn't start out that way. They came in as gung-ho individuals—and then they got their individual identities stripped away to one way, one thinking. Think of it as the difference between a mosaic (individual identities that combine to create one great picture) and a melting pot (brand identity that forces all individual identities into one undifferentiated mass). Now that their identities have been melted away, they do what they're told—and they are unprepared to do anything but pass that on to future leaders and expect their compliance. *That's why you can't expect a strategy built on personalization to immediately connect with leaders whose mindset was shaped in the age of standardization.*

Aligning Brand and Individual Identities

To shift the thinking, understanding, and buy-in, there must be a greater sense of alignment between the brand identity and individual identities. To account for the realities and values of individuals, organizations have to build enough trust so people will accept—and even welcome—being known on that level. To execute this, a workplace requires everyone to be both independent and interconnected, while at the same time it focuses on who people are and what their individual capacities are. That requires everyone to break free and understand

- how their job responsibilities must change
- how they will need to lead and communicate differently
- how they will need to listen to their associates more and recognize that the brand will need to be designed by both their employees *and* their customers
- how they will need to lead that process together, across the organization, not in some marginalized fringe position trapped in Human Resources.

Yes, that's a lot of human conversations that will need to happen. And they don't start with telling people what to do. They start with listening to who the people are, because that's what people are asking inside: *Do you know me?* That's why I start many of my presentations by saying: "I have nothing to present. My objective today is to get to know you all as individuals. Because if we don't believe we can find alignment between who we are and how we can best contribute, it doesn't matter what we are actually trying to solve for. We have to see value in individual identity. Let's have a conversation about who we are." Of course, most presentations to organizations, whether by people from the outside or on the inside, don't begin like that. Instead, they focus on the entire room as one identity. Which is exactly what that leader was doing in the scenario. His solution was basically to construct a beautifully written, heartfelt, and personalized . . . form letter.

You've probably gotten one of those (at least in an email) from someone you ostensibly care about, as well as from scammers who really don't want to execute that arrest warrant for your back taxes. Do you fall for the scam? Of course not! Then why do you expect your people to trust you when you send the same kind of email? Because you really mean it? I assure you those scammers really mean that they want your money. I'm not saying leaders like the one in the scenario are perpetrating a fraud; they were just trained in the age of standardization and have fooled themselves into thinking that they are executing leadership in the age of personalization. Those leaders are as lost and confused as their employees.

Wouldn't it just be easier to forget about the tension and messiness of individual identities and fall back into standardization, because it's really neat and efficient?

Absolutely. Put your coat on, the organization's cold.

Individual Identities and the Standardization Trap

I have sat in meetings with C-suite level people laying out brand strategies just like that leader in the scenario. They hired expensive consultants who spent weeks at the company talking to leaders, employees, and customers. Those consultants presented their findings in 120-slide decks that told the organizations exactly what they could have found out if the leaders had just talked to the people themselves and had different, more human conversations. So how do you create a culture in which you and your people can have those conversations? What most employees say they want today is to belong to a purpose and to contribute without feeling judged. We as leaders have to trust people to use their capacities and capabilities. To allow them the freedom to be empowered. Without that trust and safe space, free from judgment, they will just do what they are told to satisfy us. There's no value in fighting for what you know is right as an individual if no one truly understands its value.

For example, a senior executive doing people analytics in retail told me that all her organization wanted from the complex data was a single solution that could improve employee performance, efficiency, and service at the store level. When her team came up with a solution that could improve those things at average-performing stores in more than half the states they served, by more than 40 percent, her boss was thrilled. He then asked her to apply that same solution to every store in every state, including the poorly performing and successful stores, too. She argued that all the data showed that customer and employee bases varied from state to state and thus the standards should be different for those stores. She showed her boss that they had different *identities* that would need several solutions. He thought that was too messy—besides, a store was a store. She explained that was the attitude that got them in this mess in the first place and why they invested in people analytics. He told her she didn't understand how the company worked. So she did what she was told. It took a massive failure to prove her point, but by then she had taken a job at another company.

This story exemplifies the standardization trap that happens most clearly when dealing with individual identities. It's comparable to the idea that a wounded animal is the most dangerous animal and a line I said in Part 1: Personalization spooks standardization and when threatened, standardization fights back—hard. Falling back into standardization often happens at the first sign of trouble, be it a hit to the bottom line or even something bigger that might actually affect lives. Look no further than Boeing for evidence. After two of its 737 MAX planes crashed, killing everyone on board, the company did not do the human thing: care about the individuals flying *and ground the planes.* This was their most important jet; reputation management of the brand's identity through the plane was essential. Boeing did eventually ground them globally, but only after several countries, including the United States, grounded them—and not before losing trust and taking a huge hit in the court of public opinion in addition to its bottom line.

But don't be too quick to cast stones at Boeing. Even the most progressive organizations trying to lead in the age of personalization get it wrong. These companies get that standardization makes a company less nimble overall, while personalization enables it. They get that if you're standardized to operate in a certain way, it's harder to pivot when you need to. They get that a company that creates a culture built around personalization will be more able to respond to anything. *They get that standardization might be a good way to prepare for changes you can see coming—but that's not how change works anymore.* But then those companies let go of standardization completely, instead of finding the balance between standardization and personalization.

The goal of leadership in the age of personalization should be to unlock our capacity as individuals and bring everyone to the table to create new standards, not to avoid standards completely. Here's an example of what I mean: a national brand that has huge market position in its industry has been established in a city for two generations. Today the city is booming, and new businesses and industries are springing up all around that brand. Its talent base is ripe for the taking. But these new brands are highly entrepreneurial. They give leaders the freedom to define their own paths in order to deliver on expectations. Jobs are measured on individual productivity. The leaders hired away from the national brand are captivated by the opportunity, but those leaders have also grown up being told by the organization to put their coats on. Revenue, profits, and results were what mattered to move up to those leaders in the national brand. So when their new company says, "Go create the opportunity and figure out what it should be," it sounds like an old *Far Side* cartoon of a person talking to a dog:

> *What we say to dogs*: "Okay, Ginger! I've had it! You stay out of the garbage! Understand, Ginger? Stay out of the garbage, or else!"

> *What they hear*: "Blah Blah Ginger Blah Blah Blah Blah Blah Blah Blah Blah Ginger Blah Blah Blah Blah Blah ... "

We can't hear what we don't understand, and we don't understand because we still don't know who we are. It's impossible to lead in the age of personalization—and much easier to stay trapped in standardization—if you don't know yourself, or where you best fit, or how to optimally contribute to the evolution of the business. We're all in search of our identities to become more influential and reach success, significance, and happiness. The age of standardization used to give us that when the business defined the individual. Today, all people want to be led *and* served as individuals. They don't want to assimilate; they want to be and be known for who they really are and how they best contribute. Each of those identities—every individual—can have a unique influence on a brand or business opportunity. All that combines to create the foundation of a culture where your people know how they best contribute, and that you fully support their individual success and growth—and that they are not the source of your problems. But that's not enough to sustain that culture: Most people—even when they feel valued as individuals—are not given the opportunity to discover what this influence could be, and to contribute to their highest capacity.

Questions to Consider:
Individual Identities

- How are your/your organization's organizational processes set up to make sure consumers/clients feel seen, heard, and/or respected?

- Are any processes dedicated to getting to know consumers/clients as individuals, and to make sure that knowledge is shared—as appropriate—with the employees who interact with them (call centers, marketing, public relations, etc.)?

- Do your employee engagement indicators measure whether employees feel safe to be their whole selves at work, meaning they don't have to hide aspects of themselves from leaders or coworkers?

- How do you value individual identities and how do you avoid letting the brand identity standardize those identities?

- What keeps you up at night? Something about you, or about the brand? How do you separate the two?

PART 5

STANDARDIZATION:
MISSION
PERSONALIZATION:
CONTRIBUTION

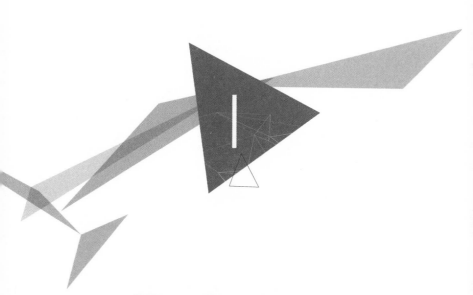

The Scenario

A company offers products to help parents and teachers make reading fun for kids. It started as a hobby of its founder—a passionate pursuit of his sincere belief that the world would be a better place and kids' lives enriched if they read more. Positive publicity, five-star customer reviews, and one viral video later, he had the start of a business. Over the next year, he worked hard and invested a lot of time and money to assemble a team that shared his belief, loved kids, and represented the different ways kids learn and teachers teach. As they built the business, they listened to and learned from each other and from schools, libraries, parents, psychologists, and of course kids themselves. The founder allowed all their feedback to shape the direction of the company. Their influence could be seen in every one of the products. As a result, "making reading fun" has become the unofficial company mission and is engrained in everyone involved. They live it and naturally sprinkle the phrase into everything from reports and presentations to sales calls and social media without even thinking about it.

- *In media interviews*: "This new line is representative of how everything we do is about making reading fun for kids."
- *In sales calls*: "All of our products make reading fun."
- *In meetings with school boards*: "We are committed to making reading fun."
- *In quarterly sales reports*: "Sales are up 10 percent and customers say our new products really do make reading fun."
- *In presentations to potential partners*: "Together we can make reading fun."
- *In social media*: "Working hard in our innovation lab today #MakeReadingFun."

With the products now selling beyond expectations and huge revenue growth projected for next year, the founder encounters organizational needs and demands he never experienced before and lacks the time to handle himself. So he makes the tough decision to step aside from the day-to-day operations to focus on product development. He will take the title of CEO and hire a chief operations officer (COO) to oversee everything from marketing and advertising to ecommerce and social media to inventory and infrastructure to accounting and new hires.

He explains to the teams why he felt the need to do this: There are new demands on everyone these days, new responsibilities, people leading who have not led before, and systems for tracking customers and products that have never been necessary. Everyone is moving a mile a minute, being pushed out of their comfort zones. He can see them struggling with the changes but also determined to succeed. The right COO can help them do that in ways he never could. He will thus step back to allow that person the space to lead and transform the organization.

The CEO spends the next weeks developing a list of candidates to interview from an executive search firm and his own network. He also encourages the team to suggest anyone they know, including themselves. After bringing in several candidates and getting feedback from the team, they choose a candidate everyone agrees can do the job. She lacks the deep experience in their industry that other candidates have, but she has the proven ability to integrate systems in rapidly growing start-ups and small businesses without, as one of her former employer's said, "destroying the magic" of the company.

The COO hits the ground running, working with the teams to bring in leadership that complements, enhances, and expands the possibilities of what they can do while applying new systems for controlling information, and automating some tasks. She challenges them to see new opportunities that the busy-ness had blinded them to. At the same time, she pursues her passion for branding, and her first initiative is to apply for a service mark to make the company's unofficial mission official: Make Reading Fun[SM]. The next day, the words appear painted on the wall behind the front desk with that [SM] at the end.

Think about this scenario through the lens of leadership in the age of personalization and the standardization of "me." How have the CEO, COO, and this organization succeeded, and how might they fall into a standardization trap?

What Does Your Organization Solve For: Mission or Contribution?

I f you haven't figured it out, the company in the scenario has been leading with personalization since it was a company of one. The founder pursued his vision and passion for making reading fun for kids. When he saw and seized an opportunity in the market for his products, he turned his side job into a business. As its leader, he embraced the idea of the standardization of me by demonstrating inclusion and allowing customers and employees to influence and define the business.

By being inclusive, his passion (to make reading fun) became a meaningful shared belief—a two-way street that reflected the individual commitment and contribution of everyone by becoming the company's unofficial mission. They don't just feel this mission, they "live it." When they speak its words, they're genuinely asking customers, partners, and each other to join together in their pursuit. They've made it their own. Making reading fun had become a meaningful movement where everyone shared a sense of ownership and contribution.

What this leader intuitively understood is that when others tell us what to do, they standardize "us." We don't have to be accountable to feeling anything, let alone a mission (no matter how great it is); we just do what we're told. **The standardization of me comes with accountability.** The more people in an organization who are accountable to that standard, the more the culture shifts to reflect individual contribution and ownership that are hallmarks of personalization.

This commitment to personalization also allowed the leader to realize the limitations of his own contributions. So as the company grew, he was willing to be vulnerable (that is, human) and admit that he didn't know what he didn't know. His business needed help— more standardization to support and scale its growth. He decided to hire a COO to do what he couldn't. That's a move that often pays off, especially in tech (think Gates and Ballmer, Zuckerberg and Sandberg). And he kept his personalization mindset through an inclusive hiring process, hiring the COO with input from the teams, allowing them influence in the decision the way he had in the products. Together they chose a COO whose individual capacity best fit the team and who could contribute to their success and eventual significance. The COO then showed through her actions that she shared the personalization mindset of the organization even as she standardized the systems and automated tasks. Then she formalized the mission they had unofficially lived for so long.[1]

So how could a company like this fall into a standardization trap? Well, like all good companies: by never seeing it coming. A need for standardization is not the same as a standardization mindset, but too many leaders turn their two-way streets of shared beliefs into one-way streets of compliance that diminish individual contribution.

Compliance Versus Commitment and Contribution

What if I told you that this scenario is based on several examples from health care, retail, technology services, finance, and more, and that most of the CEOs at those companies hired the wrong person and gave up the personalization approach to leadership? The CEOs and organizations usually went off the rails when they hired the COO. I presented a scenario that was the exception.

Here's what usually happens in scenarios like these: The CEO meets with several excellent candidates brought in by HR and/or search firms. She settles on a person she believes is a great fit based on the experience and skills that she and the organization lack. For whatever

---

[1] At this point, some might be thinking that service-marking the mission is a standardization trap. But just because you trademark or formalize something that was defined by your people doesn't indicate falling into a standardization trap. It means the opposite. It actually gives people more value and influence. This was a mission that engaged minds and hearts—it deserved to be written on the wall and owned on a more formal level. That SM throws people all the time, but it and other "marks" of standardization are not the enemy of personalization; I'd be a hypocrite if I said they were. I have trademarked Leadership in the Age of Personalization® and The Standardization of Me®, and use a service mark on Cultural Demographic ShiftSM. It's important to protect your intellectual property and what gives you distinction. That's standardization we should aspire to—and hold onto. It formally reflects the standardization of "me." It elevates the influence of individuality.

reason—from seemingly positive (not wanting to overburden the team) to definitely negative (not trusting anyone else to make the right call)—the CEO fails to allow the team the same influence in the hiring decision as it has in the products or services. The first time the team meets the COO is when the CEO announces the hire to the company, saying, "We *know* you will like him, no questions asked." *We?* Already that leader—and organization—have started to let go of a personalization mindset by denying the team inclusion and influence in the decision, the way she had in the products. Instead she expects compliance, emphasizing she "knows" they will like him, "no questions asked." This happens in large corporate organizations as much as it does small businesses. It's just scale. Instead of one CEO and one COO falling into a standardization trap, it's one influential vice president, manager, division, department, or location going off the personalization rails. And that problem can spread like a virus, infecting the leaders who *are* leading with personalization and forcing them to give up their mindset—and comply.

Much of what I just said has been touched on in the previous chapters, but let's imagine the same scenario but at a similar company. Say the COO in that company hits the ground running in branding, but instead of formalizing the company's unofficial, genuinely lived mission (Make Reading Fun^{SM}), he siloes himself with a corporate branding team he has brought in from other organizations he worked for. They emerge from their branding cocoon never having spoken to a single employee, never having asked how the employees might see the mission evolving. They never say, "Hey team, we need a bigger message for the market that broadens our mission and better connects with our customers. How do we solve for this?" Instead, the first the team hears of it is when the COO calls a company-wide meeting and announces a new service-marked mission that he says will better reflect what most companies in the industry are doing: Kids Believe Reading Is Enjoyable. We Make It That Way^{SM}.

The next day, the words appear painted on the wall behind the front desk. Then come emails, meetings, and trainings on the new mission, reminding everyone to use it—"and capitalize all words always, thanks!" The team is expected to follow—and they do. But the mission just feels like words. When people use it, their feelings begin to wane. They're no longer asking someone to join a movement like "making reading fun"; they're asking them to support the brand's identity and mission. Their once-meaningful mission was natural and easy to live and say—and helped define their connection and contribution. This new one is . . . something different. Because it came from a standardization mindset: that one-way street of compliance.

It's not hard to see what happens next. (Many of us, including me, have experienced this in organizations we work for.) The mission, lacking any influence from the team, no longer flows naturally. People sound almost robotic when they say it, because it no longer feels authentic to own it. They're just doing what they're told. Now the communications team wants to avoid it, because it no longer looks or feels like something someone actually says. Everyone sounds like they're reading from a script and thus don't really care about making reading fun. They just want to *appear* like they care. That's when the mission begins to lose its power—and even at a company like the one in the scenario, begins to look like the missions at countless companies nationwide. *The mission has become more important than individual contribution—it and the business now define the individual.*

To be clear, just as I am not anti service mark, I'm not anti mission. Every company should have a sentence or two that defines what it does and reflects the company's purpose. They can also describe how the company competes, and how it is different from its competitors. Missions are the core for creating a company's longer mission statement (what the company is, why it exists, what are its objectives, and how it will meet them) and support its core values (its philosophy, vision, culture, and direction). All of those things are important. (In *The Innovation Mentality*, I went into detail about the importance of clearly articulating your mission, goals, and corporate values, so I won't here.) But it's essential to remember that while these missions often *seem* to define a personalization mindset—*Customer service is our passion*; *Treat others with respect*; *We care about you first*—don't *most* corporate missions? After all, no one ever wrote: "Our mission is to exploit every opportunity and make money at the expense of others to enrich our shareholders and senior executives no matter what it takes—and we'll say and do anything we have to in order to make that happen, even if it means talking out both sides of our mouths!"

Hard to share in a belief like that, right? Actually, a mission like that should be easy and welcoming to people who think that way. A company with a mission like that is at least transparent about its transactional thinking and the idea that money makes us successful and significant. It's not advancing humanity—but it never claims to. If its people are authentically living that mission, it still can be demonstrating a personalization mindset—whether or not we agree with that mission. It's far more disappointing when the mission's words align with what you believe but the company fails to live that mission—even when the words of the mission do not change, when they become that standardized one-way street of compliance. The problems start when no one lives the mission, and there is no freedom for individuals to own that mission as their own and contribute in their own unique way. When the mission becomes a bunch of feel-good rules that the company says but does not live, that's standardization we must let go of.

Every organization should define its mission, but as we move from standardization to personalization, **we can't let mission define individual contribution**. That's a standardization trap.

Having a Mission Feels Good. Making a Contribution Feels Even Better.

In the age of standardization, missions had the power to define the individual. Many individuals made their brands' identities and missions their own—and were proud to identify themselves through them. That identification was so powerful it can still define their identities today, even if the industry has changed and the business is dead or almost gone. Sears was once America's "everything store" and it was everything to many of its employees back then, too. Still is, apparently. In 2018, as the retailer was shuttering its last stores, I read an article in the *New York Times* about how long-time Sears alumni regularly meet nationwide to reminisce, share war stories, and talk about how their old Kenmore appliances still run great. They shared with the reporter how the company cared about its workers, and in return for their loyalty gave them a path to the middle class. The mission may have defined them as individuals, but Sears delivered on its promises to take care of them.

Millennials and Gen Z's—and increasingly some Gen Xers—can hardly understand that mindset. Those promises today seem quaint if not impossible in retail and in many other industries and businesses. Businesses can hold onto the templates of standardization all they want, but try as they may they can't demand compliance to a mission anymore. Without inclusion and individuality, those missions are just propaganda and tools for reputation management.

In the age of personalization, employees and customers want businesses to *know* them, not *define* them. If the contribution is defined by the mission, then individuals serve the brand. Instead, they want shared beliefs and goals, and that requires respect, safety to express who they are free from judgment, and a genuine feeling that their contribution matters. People want to feel a sense of ownership. What's most meaningful to people is to know they have a chance to contribute their unique skills and strengths—no matter the mission. That's how the contribution of what we might call *individual whys* add up to growth of the "big why" of the company's goals and mission. If those individual whys are being valued and acknowledged—not assimilated—people feel fulfilled and deliver on the mission genuinely and thoughtfully. Ask yourself: *Do your people feel safe to express their passion and share their perspectives based on their personal beliefs, capabilities, values, and experiences, and do they see how those things contribute to the mission of the company?*

If your answer to that question was anything but a resounding "Yes!" your people probably feel beaten down by the weight of standardization, because standardization does not account for contribution. That's what makes it not just damaging to a personalization mindset but dangerous to morale. Companies that enable individuals to personalize the way they serve the organization's mission will create cultures that live the mission without having to write it on the wall. It will show in their employees' actions, methods, and results. It will show in the smiles as they come to work every day, feeling like themselves as individuals contributing to something greater. This could happen in even the most standardized departments and industries. I've worked with data processing units, supply chain teams, and accounting. They all tend to get this—perhaps even more than others. They touch the business every day, yet their individual contributions have been ignored for so long. These are people who need to be connected to the mission of the company and know that their contribution matters. But the larger organization just wants them connected to the mission like everyone else—to strip away their individual identities and feelings of contribution. Because missions, like standardization as a whole, often see mass variation as a threat.

Want a simple way to assess whether you are allowing your people—your customers, but especially your employees—to contribute to and help define your mission? Look at the way you give and give back. Every business today has some kind of corporate social responsibility and charitable contribution program. Is yours defined by what the organization stands for, or shaped by your individual employees—is it brand-driven or employee- and customer-directed? I'm not saying brand-driven giving isn't important, or that donating millions of dollars to great causes is not generous. Just that if it lacks any individual influence it reflects a standardization mindset. It's all fine and good for organizations to devote time and money to worthy organizations like the American Red Cross or Habitat for Humanity, but do they reflect the causes the employees care about most? If not, it's about the brand's mission, not individual contribution.

Defining where to give without listening to your people is still the business defining the individual, even if the cause is noble: "Here's what we're going to give back to and how; you follow." Companies like General Mills, Salesforce, and Subaru have learned that that is not enough in the age of personalization. You can't just define the causes to donate to or match employee donations. In the age of standardization, there were clear lines between personal and business lives. Today they are one and the same. As a result, more and more companies are extending the standardization of me to their philanthropy and allowing employee-directed giving, even paid time off for volunteering for causes most important to them. Whatever the costs are in terms of time for organizations, they know they will get a greater return on the investment from increased employee engagement and customer loyalty—and hold individual employees accountable and responsible for what they demand. Again, there is a sense of ownership. You see this all the time on a smaller scale as small retail business employees donate their tips each month to a nonprofit or a cause one or all of them get to choose.

Doesn't sound like your business? Shift your mindset from standardization (mission) to personalization (contribution) by asking one question of your people: *What do you want?* Intentionally engage them about their contributions in a way that drives value for the business. Know their individual purpose and passions. What are *their* missions?

Finding a mission has become so important in modern life that we feel like failures if we haven't identified one for ourselves and for our company. It has even become a cottage industry: People now become experts in helping other people find their passion and purpose. For some, it's their passion to help you find your passion. And that's great. I don't mean to diminish it at all. It's exhilarating if you feel a calling and work toward it. Standardization does not allow us to do this, to discover our greatness in our contribution and the power that our most authentic identities can bring. In fact, standardization has prevented leaders and employees from discovering what this greatness could be and how it can influence the organization. I refer to this influence as *what they solve for*.

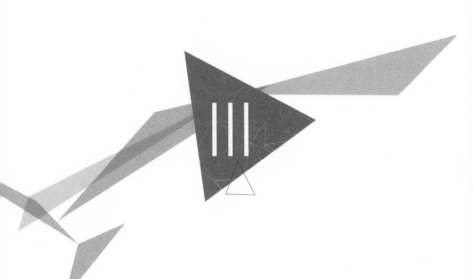

What Do *You* Solve For?

ere's a story you've probably read or heard from someone trying to demonstrate the power of having and seeing the higher calling in what you do. A person comes across three bricklayers, all working hard. He asks them what they're doing. The first one says, "I'm laying bricks." The second one says, "I'm building a wall." The third one says, "I'm building a cathedral." When others tell this story, they usually have the third bricklayer puff out his chest or exclaim his line excitedly and differently from the other two. That's because the point of the story is almost always: Look how rewarding it is to see the ultimate *why* in your work: the cathedral! That third bricklayer knows his why and the bigger why. He knows what he's working toward and that makes him proud. Love the third bricklayer because he's supposedly the difference between someone who is there to do a job, someone who sees only part of the vision, and someone who sees he's part of something more significant.

Really?

Why must we devalue the first two bricklayers and diminish their contribution? To me, they all have the same skills and are following the same plan for the cathedral. Maybe the first bricklayer just really enjoys laying bricks; he loves the process of making bricks, laying bricks, and constructing each individual portion of whatever he is building with precision and consistency. Maybe the second bricklayer is similar to the first, but always focuses on a slightly bigger picture for those bricks; he specializes in keeping walls sturdy and foundationally supportive. Maybe what both of them do excites them, too. Why does no one who tells this story have the first two bricklayers puff out their chests? Because this is a folk tale about standardization, not personalization— about the mission defining the contribution. See the bigger mission and it will define your contribution in ways that make you proud. That's a legacy of Henry Ford's assembly-line standardization of individuality to build a car faster and more efficiently than ever before. The work was undifferentiated, so he found people who found importance in their contributions to building the ultimate product, who would be proud of that and enjoy the process of doing the work: Get paid! Build a life! Bricklayers Believe Cathedral Building Is Fun!SM.

But those are not the only reasons this story doesn't work for me. My biggest problem is the story never values the deeper contribution of the bricklayers or what they solve for toward the mission of the cathedral. And what you solve for is very different from what you do.

Your Own "Why"

What you solve for is an unusual phrase and certainly not anything the metrics and KPIs from the age of standardization were ever designed to measure or value. It's deeper than a job title or description and not defined by your skills and expertise per se. It's a combination of your interests, what you stand for, and your capacity, capabilities, personal values, skills, and experiences. It's what you enjoy and consistently think about in a big way. It's how you serve others, yourself, and your purpose, and the goals, objectives, and growth of the people and organization you work for. You could call what you solve for a passion—and maybe it is. You could call it your mission, and maybe it is. But I prefer to call it something authentic that informs your individual identity.

For example, let's say you love to make people feel appreciated. You genuinely enjoy hearing perspectives that are different from yours. You aren't satisfied making a decision until you feel like you've heard every possible course of action. It bothers you when the people who should have been invited to participate in a meeting or project weren't invited. You understand the value of diversity of thought regardless of hierarchy or rank. When someone tells you about a project, your brain automatically starts connecting dots across the entire organization and you start naming other people in the company who could add value to that project, even from seemingly unrelated functions and departments. What do you solve for? You solve for inclusion.

Most organizations don't have leaders who solve for inclusion. They have people who solve for diversity. Those that do have people who solve for inclusion often do not empower them to contribute that way—or anyone else, really. Just think about the questions many leaders ask employees in interviews and reviews:

■ What are your skills and accomplishments?
■ What are your greatest strengths?
■ What do you most need to work on?

■ Where do you see yourself going?

Those questions are designed to put employees in boxes or on certain career paths, and don't give equal weight to individual capabilities and interests and how they define contribution. As a result, we simply don't know our people well enough (that is, know what they solve for) to know what they could potentially grow into. If they were hired into Department A, we start to see them as on the Department A career track, so we direct them to training opportunities that focus on skills relevant to advancing within Department A. It becomes harder for leaders to see people and their contribution beyond their Department A identity to expand their influence.

Because we don't know what our people solve for. We measure what they do; we are told to measure as defined by the company mission, leadership competencies, job descriptions, titles, and past accomplishments, not by their contributions. Consider this against what you know about the bricklayers. What if I told you the first bricklayer solves for precision, the second for resilience, and the third for vision? Would that make any of them more important than another in the story? Of course not: All those are essential to contribution and execution of the mission to build a cathedral. Yet they're not what the standardization story values. Nor what most organizations value—or leaders, in themselves or others. They want people to see value in the transactional nature of their work to support the mission, not the value of individual contributions.

Solve for the Standardization of Me

Once leaders and organizations shift their mindset to knowing what their people solve for (and it can be more than one thing), they see the contributions to their organization's success in each person's own individual way, without sacrificing the organization's mission or trying to standardize it. Leaders can then help their teams broaden their perspectives by thinking beyond themselves and their departments.

What do others solve for? Do you know? Do they know? There might be ways they can contribute that you—or they—haven't discovered yet. That's how you break down the silos of standardization and understand what distinguishes your leadership and your people, how they influence others and contribute to the mission and growth of the organization. To get started, here are my four questions using a standardization of me mindset, to help you define what you solve for.

- ■ What is unique about the way you think?
- ■ What gives you distinction as a leader/employee?
- ■ What do others expect from your presence?
- ■ What type of solutions do you consistently deliver?

Leaders who fail to understand the importance of asking, answering, and listening to the answers to these questions, and thus discovering what they and their people solve for, are the ones completely unprepared to lead in the age of personalization. They are the ones who shouldn't be leading anymore. I'm not saying they should be kicked out—maybe just placed somewhere else where their wisdom, experience, and legacies allow them to contribute differently. They have made the declaration that they are not able to change, so put them in a role that allows them to be who they are. I believe they would feel comfortable in those roles and put them in a place of contribution, too.

Leaders who do understand the importance of discovering what they solve for will thrive in ways they never imagined. As one senior executive said to me, "I used to think I needed to change myself in order to get promoted, so I could score high on the competencies being measured. But all that did was pull me away from what I could contribute." In other words, this leader was viewed as someone who would not change; all it took for him to change was to make him realize that he had the capacity to lead people the right way—his way, *the way he solved for*. Before that, he had no idea who he was. Once he began to be himself, his bosses were blown away by his transformation. They always believed in him, but there was doubt he could turn himself around. He let go of the standardization. He realized he did not need permission to influence and contribute and elevate the capabilities of others on the team. That made his bosses want him to influence more. He became the kind of leader people wanted to be around; they gravitated toward him.

Knowing what you solve for not only takes you out of a box, but also completely removes the need for boxes. It no longer matters what department, division, or team you're on. Your contribution has a broader-reaching influence that allows you to serve the mission in a more holistic way, no longer in the limited way standardization has forced you to be measured by. Knowing what you solve for allows you to feel (not just say) you have a connection to the mission of the organization and genuinely hold yourself accountable to it. Those who do not contribute based on what they solve for are the ones who need standardization, and their contributions will be short lived because they would rather assimilate to a mission that has lost its authenticity. **Significance comes when you know what you solve for.**

The bottom line is: The world of work is changing. Hierarchy/rank, job title and description, credentials and experience . . . none of that is more important than individual contributions to drive sustainable growth. Our roles, job titles and descriptions, and departments will all be less relevant in the future than what we solve for. Consider the competitive advantage for any organization using a revitalized and invigorated HR department (from Part 3), AI, and people analytics to help people figure out what they solve for, aligning that with the mission of the organization, and then allowing each individual to wield their influence and contribute to solve the organizational challenges.

When you think back to the scenario that opened this chapter and the version more like reality, what's interesting is both COOs—the one leading with personalization and the one trapped in standardization— solve for the same thing: standardization. It's just the one leading with personalization solved for the standardization of "me," the other for the standardization of "us." Remember: *Standardization is not the enemy of personalization.* The two can exist in balance as long as the leaders and their teams know what they solve for and the organization allows them to contribute to the mission. That's what the COO leading with personalization does. The COO leading with standardization tries to use the mission to influence behaviors, which causes a negative disruption that reverberates throughout the organization and disrupts the culture. Once he was given the authority to influence, he became the virus I alluded to before. He viewed anyone leading with personalization as a threat. He failed let go of the standardized approach to mission that's been written on the wall for too long.

Questions to Consider:
Contribution

- In what ways do you/your organization feel like anyone can harness their full capabilities and contribute, no matter their background (culture, heritage, gender, etc.)?

- How do leaders and employees feel and demonstrate a sense of ownership in what they do?

- Is there a way to measure how employees feel about the contribution they can make and the impact they can have on the organization? How are those contributions being valued?

- How is commitment to giving back reflective of what individuals believe in?

- Do people know what they solve for, or do they keep getting asked the same questions about strengths and weaknesses?

Stuck in Standardization

When the brand and company mission come first,
we lose the ability to see the individual impact
each of us can make.

Leadership in the
Age of Personalization

When we shift focus from brand identity to
individual identities, we invigorate our shared
missions by elevating individual contribution.

PART 6

STANDARDIZATION:
RESULTS
PERSONALIZATION:
METHODS

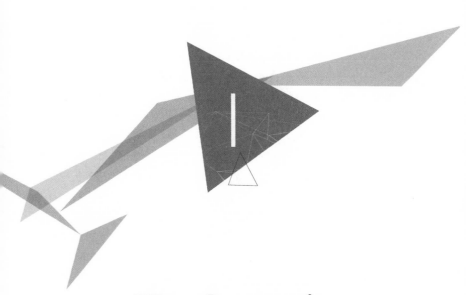

The Scenario

A farmer, well known as a magician with the soil, is approached by a land prospector from a large company. The prospector introduces himself and asks for five minutes of the farmer's time. He tells the farmer that his reputation precedes him. He asks questions about production, equipment, number of workers, revenues, and more. The farmer is happy to answer all of them. The prospector marvels at the answers and tells the farmer his reputation is well deserved: No one in the region produces as much as he does. The prospector then offers to purchase the farm for an amount that will make the farmer rich beyond any measurable standard. He adds that the farmer can still live on and work the land as an employee of the company.

"Think about it," the prospector says. "You would have the benefits of our organization's resources and efficiencies, access to the latest technologies and equipment, and be contributing to something much bigger as part of our team."

The farmer says he will think about it. The prospector asks to come back at the end of the week, and leaves behind a folder of company literature. The cover has pictures of farmers smiling in front of rows of crops that extend to the horizon, and the text touts the company's dedication to "the land and the people who work it for a better tomorrow." The farmer reads it through. He looks up stories and reviews online—mostly positive, nothing alarming. He calls a few farmers who sold to the company; all of them say the deals were exactly as the prospector described. They said they had to give up the way they'd been doing things, but the money was great—and they'd been assured that as long as they kept producing great results, there would be no concerns.

All the farmer reads and hears only reaffirms the decision he made when he first met the prospector. So when the prospector returns, the farmer politely declines his offer. The prospector tries his pitch one more time, assuring the farmer he will never get an offer like this again. The farmer again politely refuses.

The prospector turns to leave. As he does, he says, "What saddens me most is that we are now your competitor. There's plenty more land around here and its soil is the same as yours. It too can be farmed successfully. We had only hoped to include you in our great enterprise."

As the prospector drives away, one of the young farmhands who has been learning his own way with the land as he works for the farmer comes up and asks, "What the . . . *why?* You could have been a rich man!"

"You're right," the farmer says, motioning toward the farmhand's palms. "But the magic is not in the soil. It's in your hands and in mine. I did not accept his offer because he saw only what we produced. He asked nothing of how we work. He cares nothing of growing and sharing. He seeks only to reap the harvest. He and his company's money cannot be trusted."

Take a moment to consider this story through everything we have covered so far and ask yourself one question: *Whom do you want to be: the farmer or the prospector?*

II

What Are You Solving For: Sowing or Growing?

Chances are you want to be the farmer. Most people choose the farmer in this scenario. That's been true since I told a version of it in my first book, *Earning Serendipity*, and when I adapt it for keynotes and consultations. Sometimes the question I ask is whether you relate to the farmer or the prospector. Sometimes I ask who represents you most as a leader. No matter the question, the farmer is by far the more frequent choice. Yet chances are while most of us *want* to be the farmer, we're actually the prospector—and we expect the people we lead to be like him, too.

Is that so bad? Take a step back and consider the prospector. Is he so unlikeable?

- He is polite and asks questions.
- He is impressed by the farmer's results.
- He makes a generous offer.
- He is proud of his company, its mission, and the work it does; the farmer's research does not contradict this.
- He is successful, having already bought farms in the area.
- He is truthful; he keeps promises to the farmers whose farms he bought.
- He is sad the farmer says no and that he will have to compete against him.

Admittedly some of the reason that we discount these positive qualities is that the story is written to make the farmer the hero. He delivers what I usually say is the moral of this story: The prospector has forgotten the value of getting his hands dirty to establishing trust and growing deeper relationships and bigger opportunities. That's exactly why the leader gains our trust in the scenario from Part 4 based on the United Airlines commercial. (To refresh your memory: After one of his company's oldest customers fires them, the leader basically tells his team he and they have forgotten the value of getting their hands dirty by having real connections with their customers, and without ever raising his voice sends everyone, including himself, out to visit every customer. He is kind and calm as he delivers this news. He embodies the most basic definition of trust: someone reliable, good, honest, effective, and able.) In this scenario, the prospector is arguably in the same position as that leader. Yet it's the farmer who tugs on our heartstrings. Sad as the prospector may be, our hearts are on the side of the farmer. It's our heads that are on the side of the prospector.

This disconnect captures not only the tension between results and methods, but also the entire story of why standardization fails in the age of "me."

Prospecting for Results

The leader in the United commercial personifies this disconnect: He wants to lead with personalization, but his actions are all about standardization. He goes off the personalization rails by thinking since he's forgotten about the value of human connection and treating a customer with respect, everyone else must have, too. He then forces his team to comply with his methods. Nothing in that scenario shows that leader allowing people to use their individual capacities and what they solve for to contribute to solutions and find significance. His concern is the brand and the bottom line, not inclusion and individuality. He's not thinking about whether anyone else's methods matter—or if his methods are madness. He's caught in the results standardization trap: He just needs this done *now* (albeit delivering this news in the nicest way possible).

So too does the prospector personify the disconnect. Results that serve the brand—the transactions—are what drive his actions and define his success. He is so stuck in this results standardization trap that he cannot see—let alone understand—how the farmer could say no. Everything is driven by the desire to get that sale for his company. Sure, he asks questions, but all his questions are about measuring the farmer's numbers, not about the farmer himself or how his methods generated those numbers. The prospector's job is to make the farmer one of those smiling faces that reflects the company's mission. His pitch is about how the company can help the farmer with its efficiencies, technology, and equipment, not how the farmer can help define the future of the company. Not that any of that makes the prospector inauthentic or untrustworthy. He's just a trustworthy representative of standardization: He genuinely believes what he says about the benefits of the company, because the business and the results define his value.

But earning the trust of your customers and employees means something more than results in the age of personalization. **Results are about doing; they lead to success.** *Methods* **are about what you solve for; they lead to success and significance.**

Results and the actions of the prospector trace back through all the standardization words: mission, brand identity, tribal, and diversity. Methods and the actions of the farmer trace back through personalization: contribution, individual identities, human, and inclusion. The farmer values how he does things, not just the doing. And as we see in the brief interaction with his farmhand, he also values the contribution of others. He wants those who work for him to use what they solve for to develop their own methods. No way a person like that trusts the prospector. He knows he and everyone who works for him—not to mention the farm itself—will be stripped of their identities once they are folded into the company. He will be expected to comply with what the company wants. The proof is what he hears from the other farmers. They're doing exactly what the prospector said, sowing the seeds of success and "contributing to something much bigger as part of our team."

That line perfectly captures what mattered to Henry Ford and launched the age of standardization in full: delivering results that allow the company to reach its goals. If the farmer is right, then those farmers who sold will be like me in my first job: measured by how well I complied and what I delivered. Compliance was how my bosses knew I was following their rules; results were how I knew I was contributing to the success of the organization. I was prepared and trained to be highly dependent on those results for my success and happiness. While I did gain a lot in terms of understanding the methods of standardization, I felt I was losing who I was, because my way did not matter. I discovered that truth the day I thought I was going to get promoted and instead got lambasted. Why? Because I dared to visit my client the night before, rather than at six in the morning. The rules required a morning visit. It didn't matter that I thought an evening visit would lead to better results. I had no influence—they weren't preparing me to be self-directed. They were preparing me to comply. There's an old Spanish proverb, "The wise man lives off the fool and the fool lives off his job." That fool was me, letting others define who I was through results and deny me the influence of contribution by rejecting my methods. After all, who was I to question the methods? They produced results that could be measured, and a standardization mindset can only manage what it can measure—and use it to command and control individuals.

That's why the prospector says he will make the farmer rich beyond "any measurable standard" and only asks questions about things like equipment and workers, that are directly connected to results. He has no "measurable standard" for methods and doesn't understand how the farmer measures his success and significance—and the way his methods in turn contribute to the success and significance of the people he is responsible for and accountable to. So he discounts that the farmer's methods had anything to do with success. He thinks the magic is in the soil, not the humans working that soil. Humans are widgets—commodities—to the prospector and his company. They could never contribute to a greater whole and help define the business. They need to be standardized. The farmer knows his fellow farmers cashed out on more than just a plot of land. They gave up what they solved for to solve for fidelity to the brand. And as long as they deliver the results the brand measures, they can keep playing the fool.

The Tyranny of Results

To be clear, "results" is not a negative word. We should expect our people to deliver results. We can talk about methods all we want, but if those methods don't lead to results, then they're not great methods. The farmer in the scenario *does* deliver results—best the prospector has seen. That's the only reason why the prospector wants his land. The prospector must also value that the farmer works hard and has some operational standards and standardization or he never would want him to stay on after the sale. He just doesn't see that by focusing only on what he sees, he misses the bigger why behind the farmer's results. He doesn't value the *methods* that connect directly to how the farmer values his contribution and what he solves for. That's why the prospector does not try to understand what the farmer solves for. No questions about what makes him unique or what gives him distinction. He thinks the farmer solves for *results*, when in actuality the farmer solves for *growth*.

But I don't blame the prospector. Ask yourself: **When you think of results, do you think of growth, or do you think of delivering on what you're told to do?** Today's markets move so fast, and needs develop so quickly, that they blind leaders to using individual capacities and capabilities to define and then redefine the methods for seeking bigger opportunities to grow in the future. Easier to focus on getting results *now* to show progress to our daily, weekly, monthly, quarterly, and annual goals. That approach is limited and limiting. It's about generating an outcome. It's a means to an end: Doing what we're told as quickly as we can, because that's what's being measured. That's the problem with the existing metrics: They focus on what was delivered in the moment, not on potential for the future. This leads to people striving to get results but not *believing* in the way they go about getting them.

That's how results—like experience—trap leaders and their teams in standardization. The people don't see themselves in those outcomes, because only the results are valued. They don't think they can influence anything greater than the bottom line, so they stop caring about their contribution and just comply. If they're paid by the test, the call, or the transaction, they simply conduct more tests, calls, or transactions. The business model becomes centered around that. They ignore the bigger opportunities, because the organization cares little about things like customers who cannot afford your products and services *yet*. They can't take the time to help Millennials and Gen Z joining the workforce understand why the results matter, because they don't understand that themselves. They forget that those generations are growing populations in the workforce. Forget that they are the leaders of the future. Forget that they find purpose in the way they work and seek influence faster than previous generations did—and that purpose and influence could lead to bigger, better, and more sustainable results. Millennials and Gen Z are changing the way we work, and they are not engaged by standardization. And that's *their* fault? Better to dismiss their methods as madness—and, as I said in Part 3, complain how annoying they are.

But if organizations used employee engagement as a metric for success next to results, how would the results look then? Not so good, right? Because engagement is linked to methods that are linked to personalization, inclusion, individual identities, being human, and contribution. The standardization of me requires us to shift our mindset away from results to value the process as much as what that process achieves. But that won't happen if leaders keep saying they want to be the farmer but act like the prospector—and expect their people to act like the prospector, too.

I would need more than my fingers and toes to count the number of leaders I've met who were put in charge of some major initiative and told by their bosses and organization that they needed to "own the process." The leaders were excited about the opportunities to test their capacity to lead, the possibilities of putting their stamp on something important, influencing the organization, and contributing to something larger. They talked about strategies for change and bringing a different perspective to the table.

The next time I saw them, however, they sounded different. They didn't know how to do their jobs and they were freaking out about the responsibility. They still got why the initiatives are important, but they couldn't execute a strategy. Because *there was no strategy*.

They realized they were completely unprepared to be the educated, wise leaders necessary to define new strategies and methods for the initiatives and their positions. They also realized the work it would take. The responsibility of ownership required doing and solving for much more than they already did, and they were exhausted. But all that was *not* what led to them disengaging from executing leadership in the age of personalization. It was finding out that "own the process" meant "deliver results" and the organization was demanding those results *now*. Their people saw this and knew they would not get measured in any way that honored any new methods and strategies they might develop. This was when they ended up saying something to me like: "What's the point? No one is going to listen to me and it's not what I'm measured by for a promotion. None of this puts me in a greater level of influence."

One time I was hired to work with a leader who had realized this, and the first thing he said to me when we were alone was: "Just tell me what I need to do, and I'll try and get it done. If you can't, I am just going to go to someone else who can, because that's what the organization wants." With those words, the disconnect between what this leader wanted to be and actually was had been fully realized: another farmer who sold out to the company, his individual identity stripped away. He'd just do what he was told to satisfy the need of his leaders and organization. He might own his results, but that's all he owned.

That's the tyranny of results: People play not to lose instead of playing to win.

The Freedom of Methods

Essentially what I'm talking about in valuing methods is what we say we value most in America: our freedom. The farmer had the freedom to self-direct, and he refused to give it up—or take it away from his people. To do this in a traditional workplace and break free from the tyranny of results, leaders must get past the myopic linear vision of standardization and give their people freedom within a framework. That freedom is what leadership in the age of personalization and the standardization of me are all about. It's ostensibly what our country is all about. And with all the exclusive, tribal behavior surrounding our lives today, we are all, in some way, in a standardization trap.

Standardization is a framework with no freedom. It does not trust people to use their capacity and capabilities to deliver results that lead to significance—for themselves and the organization as a whole.

How many times have you sat down with members of your team individually and talked about nothing to do with results—or work at all? Just about life and aspirations, as if they were sitting on your living room sofa. If the answer is anything but "too many to count," then you either have no employees or you have not laid the foundation for anything more than results. You don't even have methods in place to be human!

Or consider this: Many companies now use intranets for employee feedback and to understand best practices and ideas the same way they use the internet for customer feedback. But what questions are being asked? Are they standardization questions like "What are we doing right? What could we do better?" Or are they personalization questions: "How can we allow your methods to better influence the direction of the organization? What methods or systems of ours stifle your ability to self-direct?" Do people see how their comments are being addressed? We think that by socializing the issues internally, we're identifying the right—or at least the better—methods that can be measured. Not if we're failing to execute leadership in the age of personalization. Is there room for leaders to listen to what people say in person? And do those people feel safe enough to speak up without fear of being judged and fear of retribution? If not, then the leaders and organization are trapped in standardization and unable to deliver on the promise of feedback. They are measuring success by the number of responses, not the methods for addressing them.

Simply put, results are the ultimate limitation on our ability to contribute—the ultimate standardization trap of outdated expectations and metrics that leads to bad leadership decisions.

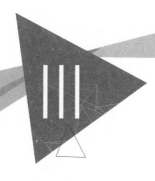

Today's Metrics Are Outdated

'm all in on leadership in the age of personalization, Glenn. But we are at the mercy of the existing metrics like the *U.S. News & World Report* rankings of universities. The criteria used for that are so outdated, but if I challenged them it would hurt our reputation and status. It would take us back two steps. So we comply with the existing metrics we don't agree with. We even spend money to advertise, even though we don't believe in these things anymore—just to make sure we stay at the place we started.

Stanford will no longer announce undergraduate application numbers in order to help reduce the focus on such data. Provost Persis Drell said, "That is not a race we are interested in being a part of, and it is not something that empowers students in finding a college that is the best match for their interests, which is what the focus of the entire process should be."

The first paragraph is part of a conversation I had with a senior administrator at a major university in August 2018. The administrator threw up his hands and told me there was nothing he could do. He wanted to lead with personalization, but he was trapped by the results expected from the status quo of standardization. The second paragraph is an announcement that appeared on the Stanford University website on the same day I had the conversation with the administrator. Stanford is doing what the first administrator wouldn't: letting go of reporting a result. Refusing to play part of the standardization numbers game. Yes, you can say Stanford has nothing to lose by refusing to play this game of results. It's Stanford. It will never have a problem recruiting the best talent and attracting the best students. But change has to start somewhere—someone has to take the first step. If it starts at the top, it has a chance to work its way down the proverbial food chain. Will other universities follow suit?

Take the First Step

So how would a results-driven organization evolve its need for results to lead in the age of personalization? By seeing it through the lens of methods first. By putting in place processes that lead to something greater than just numbers. Instead of touting your results, remember what you did in math and science classes in school and show your work. Try this exercise.

- ■ Gather the team and tell them each to identify a big result they want to achieve. Say you will meet back a week later for them to report on them.

- Encourage collaboration across the team and outside it, but don't mandate it.
- During the week, set up a meeting with each team member specifically and completely devoted to asking and answering questions, brainstorming approaches, and coaching them on strategies.
- In the meeting a week later, have everyone share the methods they used to identify what they wanted.
- Talk about what worked and what did not. Listen to what everyone has to say.
- Make sure everyone asks one good question that leads to understanding different perspectives, not to judgment of the methods.

What this exercise does is open leaders and their teams up to understanding their capacity, who they are, and how they work. They learn from each other, and not only own the methods that will make the whole team stronger but also influence other teams and departments across the organization. Your team now becomes something more than successful. It becomes *significant*. Success is achieving results through methods—competencies, values, behaviors—that were determined for you and that you did not influence. Significance is achieving the result through methods that were influenced by individuality—by what you solve for, by your purpose in support of the organization's goals and objectives

Even a sales and revenue driven organization can be about more than how much it made on a sale if its leaders care about the people and the methods they used to get those results. For example, I spoke to a sales leader at a company that used to be trapped in standardization. She told me things improved when they ditched the mandatory 9-to-6 work day and relaxed the dress code. But she told me the biggest shift was when they stopped measuring their days by how many sales they closed, but instead by how many great conversations they had. That's how new and better metrics are discovered. Her team, already the most successful in the organization, had a 25 percent increase in revenues the following quarter and has grown every quarter since. All because she took the first step to measure the methods, not reinforce the old results-based approach.

Let's go back to the administrator and the Stanford provost's quote. Who do you want to be? The administrator knows the age of standardization is failing and why there is such a need to embrace the Age of Personalization. Yet he still uses the outdated templates that force universities to comply with the standards. He focuses on reputation management, the way leaders in every industry do. He doesn't want the "perception" of their brand to be compromised—better to bow to the metrics of standardization. Doesn't matter how outdated they are. Better to follow them so he doesn't get a bad performance review, or fired. That mindset also prevents him from asking if the perception of the university might be *enhanced* by rebelling against the old metrics, as a result of the Cultural Demographic Shift and the rise of the Millennial and Gen Z generations. That's what Stanford did. What are you doing?

The first step toward getting rid of old metrics and creating new ones that are influenced by personalization is a leap of faith, for sure— even more so when you have dozens, hundreds, and thousands of people spread out across a dizzying employment tree filled with siloed departments contentedly delivering results. Many of the leaders of those silos are very comfortable and happy with the status quo. They will always be the resistance when any new methods appear. These people who are often of greatest influence always resist the change—they are the people most unprepared to lead. They know if the organization reinvents itself and they don't, they will either be unqualified for their job or they will become extinct. They stopped taking any steps forward a long time ago. It's time for them to step up, move over, or go. The longer they stay, the longer those outdated metrics not only define them and their people, but also distance them from what they solve for.

We just can't keep working with the same metrics we did a generation ago. Leaders awakening to this see that methods are now more important than results. Why and how a focus on results stifles individuality, as the prospector's company would do to the farmer. They are so connected to the metrics. Outdated metrics prevent new thinking and solutions, because new thinking and solutions don't align with the metrics. The metrics shouldn't tell you what to do. They should *guide* you, not cloud your decision making. We must stop being enslaved by the metrics. Take the first steps out of your standardization bondage.

As I was about to take the first step into this book, I remembered how hard those steps can be. I knew I was trying something different with its creation, as part of the reinvention of my business. But it is so easy to slide back into standardization. So easy to use the existing templates and what worked in the past. So easy to just do nothing and not reinvent what you are doing, just sow the seeds of results like the prospector, not be the farmer and keep growing. But if I was not willing to challenge convention, I would be a hypocrite. The process has been exhausting but energizing. It made me feel sorry for those leaders so beaten down by standardization, so unable to define and redefine who they are.

Are you ready? I can't tell you how to find your how, but I hope I have helped you understand why shifting your mindset to leadership in the age of personalization and the standardization of me is so important in our world today. There are too many people out there telling us to fear inclusion, fear individuality, manage difference by excluding it. Because exclusion is easier than inclusion, tribalism easier than being human, hate is easier than love. That's why people eye someone like me with suspicion. Conservatives think I'm a squishy liberal. Liberals think I'm trying to save old white guys. All because I'm not trying to take anything away or push anyone out. I'm trying to bring us together to find a way forward in business, the way our politics cannot.

And if after all we've covered, you agree and feel you are ready to take the first step into truly executing leadership in the age of personalization, let me be the first to say *We've been waiting for you.* As the farmer said, the magic is not in the soil. It's in your hands and in mine. It's time to start being who we want to be.

Questions to Consider:
Results

■ How is your organization trapped in the tyranny of results? If it isn't, how are people given the freedom to avoid it?

■ Do you/your organization have any metrics for measuring methods, not just results? When were any of the metrics you use last revised?

■ Look around your organization: Who is the prospector and who is the farmer? What makes them one or the other? How is each influencing (or not influencing) the organization— and you?

■ Can you think of an example of when the organization asked a question to learn about how an employee or customer accessed and/or experienced your products/ services, and then applied that lesson to the way those products/services are delivered?

■ What strategies are in place for engaging with employees and customers beyond results or information related to the specific product or service they get?

The Luxury of Time Is Over

Leadership in the age of personalization is the ultimate abundance mindset: the genuine desire for everyone to thrive individually and inclusively—success *and* significance for all. Sure, we can win by making others lose. By excluding them. By seeing "them" as a threat to "us." By stripping away who they are. By denying them the purpose they seek. By caring more about hierarchy, status, and the status quo. And in doing that, we can keep losing ourselves in the process. We can keep going at each other. Keep attacking the slightest transgression against our tribe. Keep blaming. Keep treating others as unequal. Keep losing who we are as individuals, and our care for and responsibility to our world and each other. Keep being disconnected, exhausted, and unprepared to lead.

That's what happens simply by refusing to let go of the standardization that has defined us for so long. That's just what Jillian Searle *did not do* in the story that opened this book. As the waters of the typhoon rushed around her that morning in Thailand, she did what every instinct told her to do as a parent: hold on tightly to her two young children. *Don't* let go. But then—unprepared by any experience for the choice she had to make—she got past her exhaustion and fear, shifted her mindset, and let go of one of her children. She knew the only way she could save them both and herself was to let go. She had no idea if she and her younger son would survive. When they did, she had no idea if her older son had survived. But he did. They all did. And so will we—if we learn to do the same for our children and let go.

It's time to start over. Business and life in general move faster and are more integrated than ever before. Time is compressing. We're always connected. Always on. We are a nation burning out at work— not just because we're working so hard and so much, but because we're doing that without any sense of who we are and any connection to what we are doing. Engaged or not, the negative forces of standardization have stripped so many of us of our identities. Only by rediscovering who we are as individuals and embracing that individuality in others can we find our purpose and contribute to a healthier whole.

Leadership in the age of personalization and the standardization of me are the forces that will push us to start over again. The "one way" of standardization stands in our path, suppressing all aspects of personalization: inclusion, individual identities, contribution, and methods that define who we are. Standardization may give us a sense of belonging, but it's tribal and stifles our humanity, especially toward anyone we perceive as "not me," or rather "not us." It's time to let go of the artificial hope that a single-minded devotion to one person, one group, or one way of thinking about and doing things can solve our identity crisis. We continue to disappoint and defeat ourselves through false hopes and expectations. It's time to stop fighting each other to reclaim our status, and start embracing the messiness of understanding and including others who may not share our points of view—so we all can find significance in what we contribute.

Leadership in the age of personalization and the standardization of me create healthy, sustainable environments that allow us to find that significance—that *purpose*. They propel us to be inclusive, human, and to contribute to something bigger than ourselves as individuals. They will not only define and redefine the future for the health of organizations and the economy, but will also hold us accountable to and responsible for the financial, physical, and mental health of ourselves and every individual in our communities.

All that is easier to say than do, but it takes only two words to get started. Just two words: *Let go*. The first words of this book asked a question: What are we holding onto? I'm going to ask that question again in these last words with one small word change: What are *you* holding onto?

The luxury of time is over. The waters of change are rushing around us. Our children need us to decide if we will hold onto what we know or let go and face the future to reclaim and sustain our humanity.

Let go.

Stuck in Standardization

Strict lists of expected results make us compliant and constrained—we don't feel free to explore. We play to not lose, rather than play to win. When our individual capacity is stifled, we stagnate.

Leadership in the Age of Personalization

When we loosen our grip on results and activate methods for leading in a way that honors our Age of Personalization, we become healthy. When we're healthy, we grow.

An Anthropologist's View on the Age of Personalization

Human experience and our interconnectedness are at the foundation of my approach and identity as an anthropologist. That said, I have good news and bad news for our transition to what Glenn calls the age of personalization. The bad news is that even though we're more interconnected than ever before, anxiety and conflict are rising like never before. The good news is that this hyper-interconnectedness is not the problem; it's *how* we're using the technologies that help us connect. Whether trains, planes, and automobiles that get us to each other, the 1s and 0s going though time and space that power AI and social media, or the digital rewriting of our DNA, technologies themselves are value neutral. They are neither bad nor good. They just are. It's when humans program and deploy them that they stoke anxiety and conflict, which drive us apart rather than unifying our differences into an interconnected web of interdependence—our humanity.

The technologies that connect us are just the evolution of tools like hammers: We can build with them or we can use them to destroy. Standardization in our hyper-interconnected age undermines the interdependent resilience of our humanity. It puts us in silos—echo chambers of thoughts with which we are already aligned—and limits the possibilities and opportunities of what Glenn calls "the standardization of me" and I call "cognitive diversity." In fact, standardization not only undermines our possibilities and opportunities, but makes us think we are doing personalization. Genuine personalization and cognitive diversity should allow us to bring out the best in us individually and collectively, but that is not what is happening. Instead we use the tools we have to stifle difference and segregate ourselves. That's what standardization does—through Facebook or the latest advances in AI: It casts an illusion of personalization under the guise of efficiency.

There is a parallel here with my work in international plant breeding and seed production. When humanity faced an existential food crisis in the mid-twentieth century and couldn't grow enough to feed our growing population, scientists took a standardized approach instead of a diverse and varied seed production strategy. Rather than creating and maintaining a seed portfolio of plant varieties adaptable to a wide range of dynamic growing conditions, scientists created "superseeds," otherwise known as modern or improved varieties, that could grow anywhere in the world and outperform any other seeds on the planet. And after we standardized seeds . . . we standardized the people who grew them. We transformed farmers into mass consumers rather than individual creators of seed. Farmers lost their artisan legacy and joined the assembly line.

Locally-based seed portfolios are the definition of personalization in the world of plant breeding and seed production. Adapted to the unique dynamics and resources of local ecologies, their yields are modest but steady relative to modern varieties. Conversely, the standardization of seed, increases yields and reduces biodiversity in the name of efficiency—but to achieve these improved yields, growers also have to standardize their fields with inorganic, nonlocal inputs like fertilizers, herbicides, and pesticides. This standardization of seed has us growing more food today than we ever have, and we're doing this with fewer farmers. Yet remarkably, world hunger and food insecurity are rising. With the standardization of seed, we achieved "efficiency," but we failed to accomplish the goal that motivated us in the first place: feeding the planet.

Simply put, superseeds streamlined our food production but at the cost of people's identities as instrumental and interdependent resources for resilience. Think about this in terms of crayons. When I got my first box of 64 crayons as a kid, a world of color opened up to me. No matter what coloring book I had or picture I wanted to draw, the potential to express myself blossomed when I had 64 choices instead of the 8-pack I had been using. I didn't know what pictures I'd be coloring in the months to come, but I was ready for whatever would come my way because I had the strength of 64 choices, *including the eight I had before.* This is not what we are doing with seed. This is not what we are doing with people in offices. We are making smaller and smaller boxes of crayons when deep down, everyone is longing for a 64-pack.

I know we can make money in the short term with a simpler product and uniformity. But there are long-term costs associated with reducing our cognitive and physical diversity—and our ability to stand up for it. The strength of a biologically diverse food system is our strength for the future, not something to be streamlined or eliminated. The strength of leadership in the age of personalization is the same for the cultures we create at work. We need cognitive diversity for resilience and innovation.

We can't be threatened by personalization. We can't see "culture" as static. Culture is the way people do things together. Not the same—*together.* The contested areas between and within cultures allow us to adapt, innovate, and grow, individually and collectively as humans. Will we continue to eliminate personalization through standardization? That path is the slow death of humanity. The slow death of our cognitive diversity. The slow death of individuality and inclusion—the things that define the personalization about which Glenn speaks. Interconnectedness doesn't require cognitive diversity, interdependence does. But right now, interconnectedness is nothing but a surface-level illusion of personalization—of the human connection that should unite us, not drive us apart.

—Scott M. Lacy
Associate Professor of Anthropology at Fairfield University
Founder & Executive Director of African Sky (*www.africansky.org*)

Take the Assessments: Know Your Starting Point

We've all been influenced by standardization, perhaps in ways we're not even aware of. To help you see how, GLLG offers free assessments that have been taken by tens of thousands of leaders and employees worldwide. These assessments are designed to help you take inventory of yourself, your team, and your organization. The insights from the data you get will help you see where you are limited and trapped by standardization, and help you be more strategic in your approach to leadership in the age of personalization and the standardization of "me," to build inclusive, high-performance teams that get out in front of change and uncertainty. Taken together, they hit all the points covered in this book.

- Allowing individuality and influence: Create teams of individuals that function together as part of a healthy whole.
- Driving growth and evolution: Make leaders and teams who are clear about what they solve for and how they influence the future of the organization.
- Having a human culture full of shared purpose and beliefs: Find like-mindedness in differences, not forced assimilation.

Leadership in the Age of Personalization Assessment

This tool will help you identify where you are stuck in standardization and how you can find your way out, to lead more effectively in this Age of Personalization.

Workplace Serendipity Assessment

It all starts with opportunity management, because yes, opportunity takes management. This assessment will measure your team proficiency in opportunity management, based on four critical skills that help you to *earn serendipity*—a term we coined to represent opportunity management, innovation, and the advancement of humanity.

Diversity of Thought Assessment

Diversity of thought in the workplace is one of the most powerful competitive advantages for our workgroups and organizational teams. This assessment will measure your teams' openness to diversity of thought, based on the individuals' self-awareness and their approach to relationships and leadership influence.

Inclusion as a Growth Strategy Assessment

The US population is more diverse than ever. Minorities are becoming majorities. Differences are the new normal. This assessment was designed to measure your organization's readiness for the Cultural Demographic Shift[SM] in order to lead inclusion as a growth strategy. It measures twenty-three key indicators in four critical areas: Enterprise Leadership; Workforce Representation; Consumer Experience; and Population Health.

You can find links to all of these at: https://www.glennllopis.com/people-analytics/.

Just remember: Not everything human can be optimized through data—and looking at the data you get from these assessments is no replacement for talking with and listening to people.

Personalization in Practice: My Trilogy

The book in your hand is my third—and I originally had no plans to write it. But working closely with leaders and teams at some of the largest organizations in the world and hearing their frustration and exhaustion, I knew I needed to do more. They've felt restricted their entire professional lives, and they wanted to be free to be who they are and empower others to contribute. These were leaders and organizations trapped in standardization mindsets. They needed to let go and shift those mindsets to personalization and the standardization of "me." And they needed help getting there. I realized this is what I solve for: I help people escape the traps of standardization, reclaim their identity so they can have influence, and help those they lead do the same. That's how *Leadership in the Age of Personalization* was born and completed a trilogy that helps you reclaim individuality and drive inclusion as a growth strategy for the betterment of your organization, institution, team, family—whomever and whatever you serve.

My first book, *Earning Serendipity: 4 Skills for Creating and Sustaining Good Fortune in Your Work*, is about personalizing your own path to significance. Most positive changes in fortune are no mystery. We all have control over the path to prosperity. Progression along that path is the result of a rare combination of skills that readers can develop and apply in their careers, businesses, and lives. I call them the four skills of opportunity management:

- *See* with circular vision.
- *Sow* entrepreneurial seeds.
- *Grow* seeds of greatest potential.
- *Share* the harvest of your success to re-sow significance.

My second book, *The Innovation Mentality: Six Strategies to Disrupt the Status Quo and Reinvent the Way We Work*, is about learning how to activate individuality to build high-performance leaders, teams, and a culture of inclusion throughout an organization. Leaders learn to take ownership of a new mindset—the innovation mentality—and implement six essential strategies designed to disrupt the status quo, reinvent the way they work, and leverage the full potential of their workplace cultures, employees, teams, partnerships, and client and consumer relationships:

- See opportunity in everything.
- Anticipate the unexpected.
- Unleash your passionate pursuits.

- Live with an entrepreneurial spirit.
- Work with a generous purpose.
- Lead to leave a legacy.

Why we need to do the things I laid out in those first two books is what *Leadership in the Age of Personalization* is about, and they're all connected in a single equation:

$$\frac{\text{Earning Serendipity} + \text{The Innovation Mentality}}{\text{Leadership in the Age of Personalization}}$$

Complete the equation and you not only understand why standardization fails in the age of me, but also how to reclaim what all of us need: our humanity. But none of that happens unless you own your identity and know what you solve for. This is what my father told me to do me when I struggled at my first job: never forget who I was as an individual. Not let anyone or anything else define it—*own it.* My father's advice prepared me to go through the filters of life staying and being healthy, no matter the ups and downs of business or the uncertainties in life. All because I managed my identity, and as a result became more vulnerable and open-minded and wise enough to let people influence me—and in return I influenced others to do the same. This book is the culmination of that journey and is my father's legacy as much as mine. My hope is that it helps you own your own legacy, too.

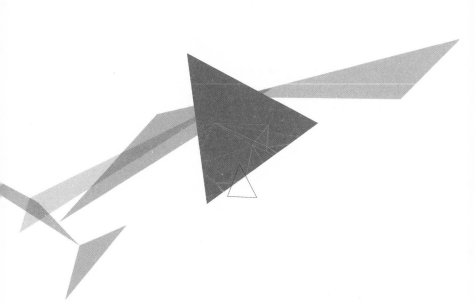

Acknowledgments

My Family

My wife, Annette: I could have never written this book without you. You give me strength, fuel my faith, and have taken my perseverance to places it's never gone before. Thank you for your love, patience, and understanding. I love you.

My daughter, Annabella: You are my ultimate inspiration. Never let go of your identity. It will help you find your purpose and live a life of joy and happiness. I love you.

My father, Frank: I miss you, Dad. Thank you for knowing me before I knew myself. Your wisdom and guidance helped me navigate life's uncertainties and allowed me to trust myself and help others in the process. You were the perfect father. I love you.

My mother, Jenny: You passed your tenacity and entrepreneurial spirit on to me. Without these gifts I could have never accomplished my dreams in life. I love you.

My brother, Eric: Thank you for always knowing how to set the bar for excellence. It's an honor to be your little brother. I am proud of you and what you have become. I love you, bro.

My sister-in-law, Taj: You have always been the voice of reason. Your class and dignity shine a brighter and healthier light on the entire family. Thank you for being such an amazing wife and mother. I love you.

And to Marina, Isabel and Nic: I am so proud of you! I love you.

The GLLG Leadership Team

To Guilherme Oliveira: Thank you for pushing me to be my best—and for helping me understand what best means in the age of personalization. It's because of your leadership, and the authentic individual that you are, that I am better prepared for the future.

To Jim Eber: Thank you for giving my thinking deeper meaning, understanding, and impact. You've elevated my thought leadership and taken it to new heights. I will be forever grateful.

Kim Perez: Thank you for the manner in which you have simplified my thinking and words, which are now more powerful than ever. You are masterful.

Sandy Sickler: Thank you for caring so much and for having my back. You've always had our clients' best interests at heart. I appreciate your belief in our journey, and your daily spirit.

Paulo Silvano: Thank you for creating an identity for GLLG. Your passion for design and eagerness to learn is infectious. Your talent will continue to flourish and inspire others to do the same.

And to all our GLLG clients: Thank you for trusting me and the team, embracing our identity while putting yours in our hands. Together, we can build a healthier whole for our children and ourselves. Together, we can build a better future.

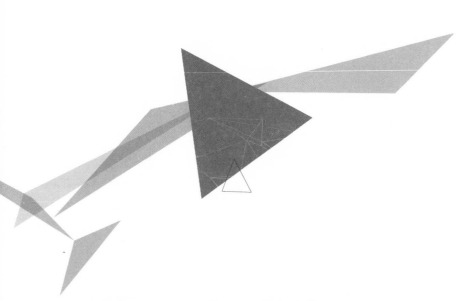

About the Author

Glenn Llopis (pronounced 'yō-pēs) is the chair of the Glenn Llopis Group (GLLG), a nationally recognized workforce development and business strategy consulting firm, specializing in Leadership in the Age of Personalization®.

A bestselling author of the books *The Innovation Mentality* and *Earning Serendipity*, Glenn has more than twenty-five years' experience as an executive and entrepreneur. He is a senior advisor and speaker to Fortune 500 companies and organizations, ranging from retail to consumer packaged goods to health care. Known for helping organizations move inclusive leadership to where it belongs—in corporate strategy and transformation—he helps leaders at those companies disrupt the status quo and reinvent the way they work.

Glenn is a contributing writer to *Forbes*, *Harvard Business Review*, *Entrepreneur* magazine, and *Huffington Post*. His writings, speaking engagements, and consulting assignments focus on operationalizing and leading growth in the Age of Personalization. He was recognized as a Top 20 Influential Writer by *Forbes* and a Top 100 Leadership Speaker and Business Thinker by *Inc.* He has been featured as a business leadership expert on CNN, Fox News, Bloomberg, Univision, ABC, NBC, and CBS.

A UCLA graduate, Glenn fast-tracked at the Gallo Wine Company and at Sunkist, where he became the youngest executive in the company's 100-year history. Leading the successful turnaround of Sunkist's juice beverage division opened the door for his next endeavor—at only age 30—as a senior executive at American Seafoods Company. The result was an increase in market share, new brand introductions, and a full-scale transformation of the company. Glenn then went on to form his own successful food business before transitioning into his current role.

Glenn is a member of the World Innovation Network (WIN) and serves on the advisory board of the Brittingham Social Enterprise Lab at the Marshall School of Business at the University of Southern California. He is a board member of Lion's Heart, a national, nonprofit community service organization for teen volunteering and leadership, and a mentor for Junior Achievement. He is also a member of the exclusive Renaissance Weekend think tank. He lives in California with his family.

Leadership in the Age of Personalization

When we turn diversity into inclusion, we stop being tribal and start seeing each other as human.

When we shift focus from brand identity to individual identities, we invigorate our shared missions by elevating individual contribution.

When our individual capacity is stifled, we stagnate. But when we loosen our grip on results and activate methods for leading in a way that honors our Age of Personalization, we become healthy. When we're healthy, we grow.